The
Bar/Bat
MITZVAH
PARTY
Table Plan
Book

Alison McNicol

First published in 2014 by Kyle Craig Publishing
Text and illustration copyright © 2014 Kyle Craig Publishing
Design: Julie Anson

ISBN: 978-1-908707-31-4
A CIP record for this book is available from the British Library.

A Kyle Craig Publication
www.kyle-craig.com

Introduction

Welcome to the Bar/Bat Mitzvah Table Plan book!

Congratulations on your forthcoming big day– you now have some very exciting times ahead, and I'm sure you can't wait to get started planning your Mitzvah party!

Creating the guest list for a special party can at times feel like an overwhelming task; deciding who to include, who to leave out, sticking to the number of guests that your budget allows for and keeping all your family and friends happy – it's not easy!

And then, just as you finally decide on the guest list comes the fun part – deciding who sits where!

Creating the perfect table seating plan for your Mitzvah Party can be a complicated task– lots of trial and error – swapping around aunts, cousins, relatives and friends to create that perfect mix of guests at each table. But how to arrive at the perfect mix?

Forget about improvising with post-it notes and names on bits of scrap paper, or even downloading and figuring out complicated computer programs – here's the fun and easy 'old-skool' way to plan your perfect party table seating plans!

Remember those cut out and dress-up dolly books? Well imagine if you could cut out each table in your room layout? Then cut out and fill in the name cards for all of your guests. Then move them around as you play around with all the different options? Much more fun!

Turn the stressful task of organising your perfect Mitzvah Party table seating plan into a fun game!

Mazel Tov!

Guest List

Use these pages for the first draft of your potential guest list. Feel free to photocopy in case you need to make several edits!

Family

---------------------- ---------------------- ---------------------- ----------------------

---------------------- ---------------------- ---------------------- ----------------------

---------------------- ---------------------- ---------------------- ----------------------

---------------------- ---------------------- ---------------------- ----------------------

---------------------- ---------------------- ---------------------- ----------------------

---------------------- ---------------------- ---------------------- ----------------------

---------------------- ---------------------- ---------------------- ----------------------

---------------------- ---------------------- ---------------------- ----------------------

---------------------- ---------------------- ---------------------- ----------------------

---------------------- ---------------------- ---------------------- ----------------------

---------------------- ---------------------- ---------------------- ----------------------

---------------------- ---------------------- ---------------------- ----------------------

---------------------- ---------------------- ---------------------- ----------------------

---------------------- ---------------------- ---------------------- ----------------------

---------------------- ---------------------- ---------------------- ----------------------

---------------------- ---------------------- ---------------------- ----------------------

---------------------- ---------------------- ---------------------- ----------------------

---------------------- ---------------------- ---------------------- ----------------------

---------------------- ---------------------- ---------------------- ----------------------

---------------------- ---------------------- ---------------------- ----------------------

---------------------- ---------------------- ---------------------- ----------------------

---------------------- ---------------------- ---------------------- ----------------------

---------------------- ---------------------- ---------------------- ----------------------

---------------------   ---------------------   ---------------------   ---------------------
---------------------   ---------------------   ---------------------   ---------------------
---------------------   ---------------------   ---------------------   ---------------------
---------------------   ---------------------   ---------------------   ---------------------
---------------------   ---------------------   ---------------------   ---------------------
---------------------   ---------------------   ---------------------   ---------------------
---------------------   ---------------------   ---------------------   ---------------------
---------------------   ---------------------   ---------------------   ---------------------
---------------------   ---------------------   ---------------------   ---------------------
---------------------   ---------------------   ---------------------   ---------------------
---------------------   ---------------------   ---------------------   ---------------------
---------------------   ---------------------   ---------------------   ---------------------
---------------------   ---------------------   ---------------------   ---------------------
---------------------   ---------------------   ---------------------   ---------------------
---------------------   ---------------------   ---------------------   ---------------------
---------------------   ---------------------   ---------------------   ---------------------

Friends

---------------------   ---------------------   ---------------------   ---------------------
---------------------   ---------------------   ---------------------   ---------------------
---------------------   ---------------------   ---------------------   ---------------------
---------------------   ---------------------   ---------------------   ---------------------
---------------------   ---------------------   ---------------------   ---------------------
---------------------   ---------------------   ---------------------   ---------------------
---------------------   ---------------------   ---------------------   ---------------------
---------------------   ---------------------   ---------------------   ---------------------
---------------------   ---------------------   ---------------------   ---------------------
---------------------   ---------------------   ---------------------   ---------------------
---------------------   ---------------------   ---------------------   ---------------------
---------------------   ---------------------   ---------------------   ---------------------
---------------------   ---------------------   ---------------------   ---------------------
---------------------   ---------------------   ---------------------   ---------------------

Planning Your Seating

Once you have agreed on the final number of guests, the next step is to talk to your venue on the types and number of tables that they have. Or, if you are organizing your own table hire for your own venue or using a marquee, you will want to decide on which tables to use and how to best arrange them. Will you go for round tables or rectangular, or a mix of the two? And how will you lay them out within the space available?

Have a look at the following pages for some ideas for room layouts.

Here are some points to consider:

• What shape is the room?

• Keep walkways to the bar, dancefloor and exits clear

• Elderly guests may prefer to be seated close to the nearest toilet exit

Round tables

5' round to seat 8   5' round to seat 10   6' round to seat 10   6' round to seat 12

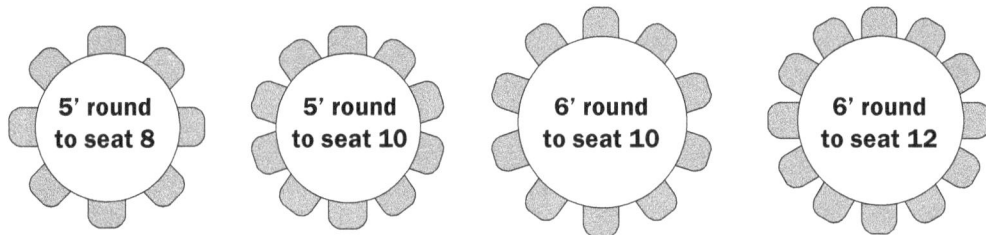

Rectangular tables

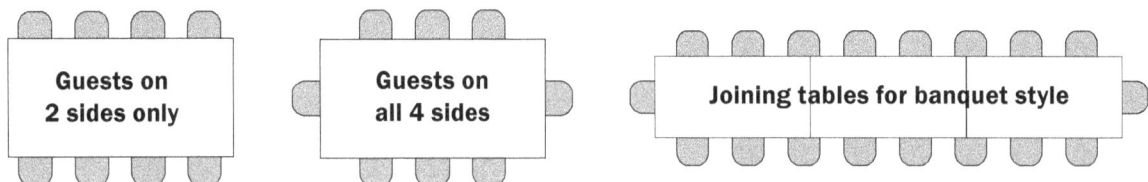

Guests on 2 sides only   Guests on all 4 sides   Joining tables for banquet style

Number of Guest Tables	Tables seating 8	Tables Seating 10	Tables seating 12
6	48	60	72
8	64	80	96
10	80	100	120
12	96	120	144
14	112	140	168

Round Tables

Number of Tables	Curved	Staggered	Around The Dancefloor
10	MAIN TABLE	MAIN TABLE	MAIN TABLE
12	MAIN TABLE	MAIN TABLE	MAIN TABLE
14	MAIN TABLE	MAIN TABLE	MAIN TABLE
16	MAIN TABLE	MAIN TABLE	MAIN TABLE
20	MAIN TABLE	MAIN TABLE	MAIN TABLE

Rectangular Tables

Number of Tables			
10	MAIN TABLE	MAIN TABLE	MAIN TABLE
12	MAIN TABLE	MAIN TABLE	MAIN TABLE
14	MAIN TABLE	MAIN TABLE	MAIN TABLE
16	MAIN TABLE	MAIN TABLE	MAIN TABLE
20	MAIN TABLE	MAIN TABLE	MAIN TABLE

Other Table Layouts

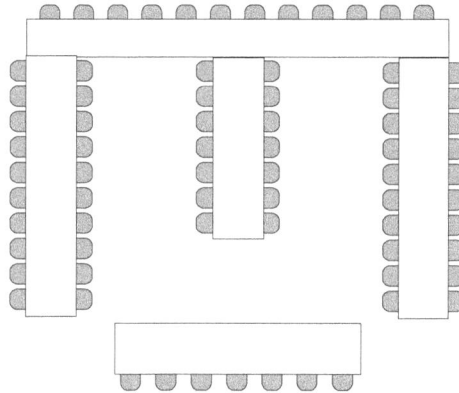

Tables in an E formation

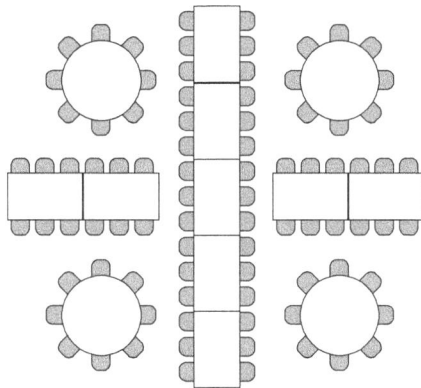

Mix of Tables Cross Shape

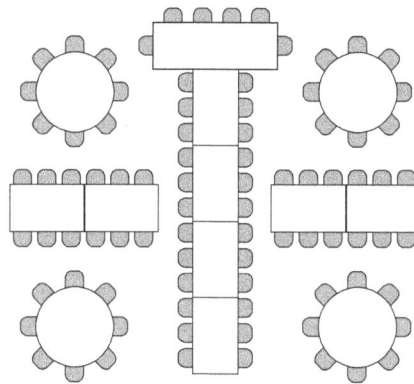

Main Table at Head of Cross Shape

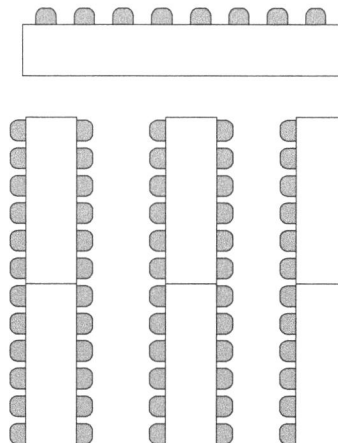

Long Rows of Tables

How To Use The Pages In This Book

Once you have your guest list completed and have decided on the shape and number of tables at your venue, it's time to start planning your seating arrangements. Now the fun can begin!

You will need

- Flat surface – table or floor, to spread your pieces out on
- Scissors
- Pen or pencil

Lets Get Started

1) Decide on what tables you will be using at your venue – round or rectangular - and cut out all the tables you will need. Feel free to copy some pages if you will have more than 200 guests.
   (The rectangular tables can be cut to size – so if you only have 6 or 8 per table, you can simply trim the table templates provided).

2) Lay your paper tables out in the room layout you prefer.

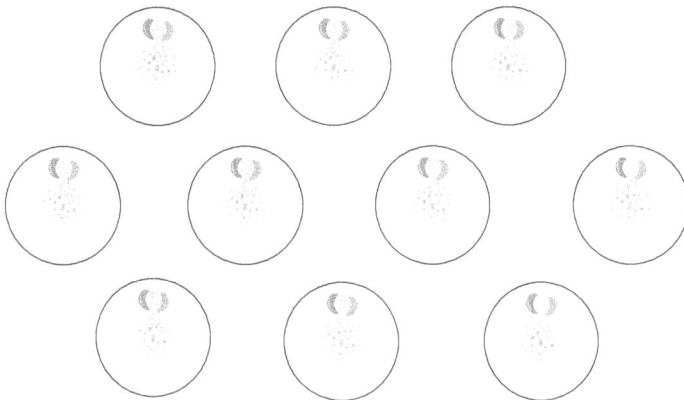

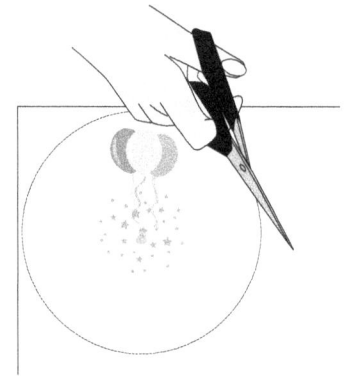

3) Fill in all your guests names on the little blank name cards, then cut out each individual namecard.

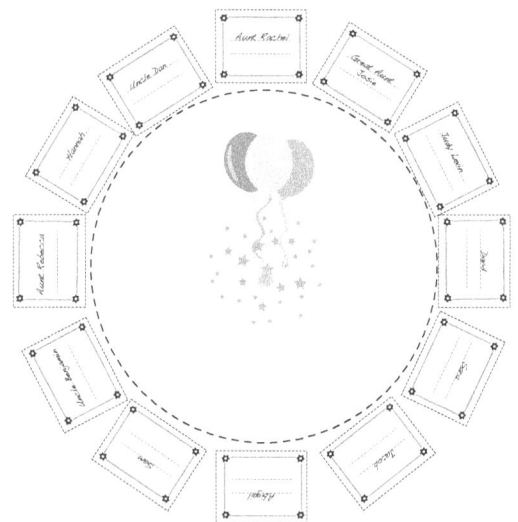

4) Start laying the names around the tables

5) Now number each table, and copy the names you have decided onto the lists on the pages at the end of this book.

6) Use the final page to sketch the final table layout, including table numbers.

Other Tables
To Cut Out

Food Table

The Bar

Gift Table

Cake Table

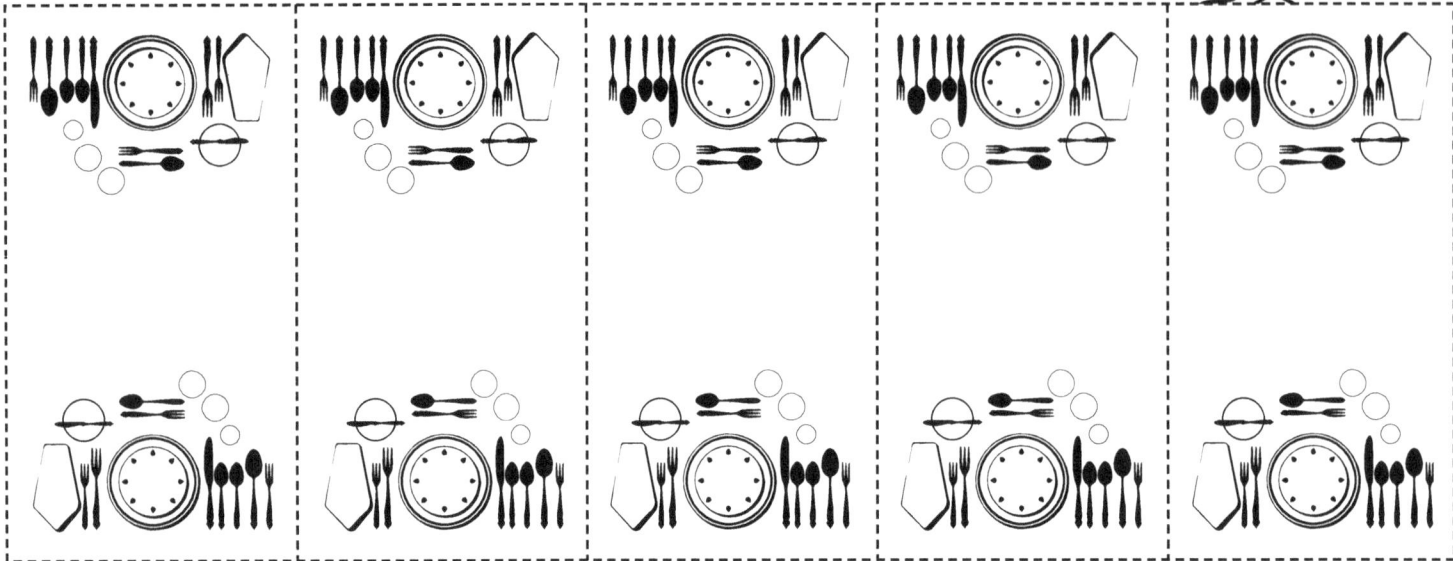

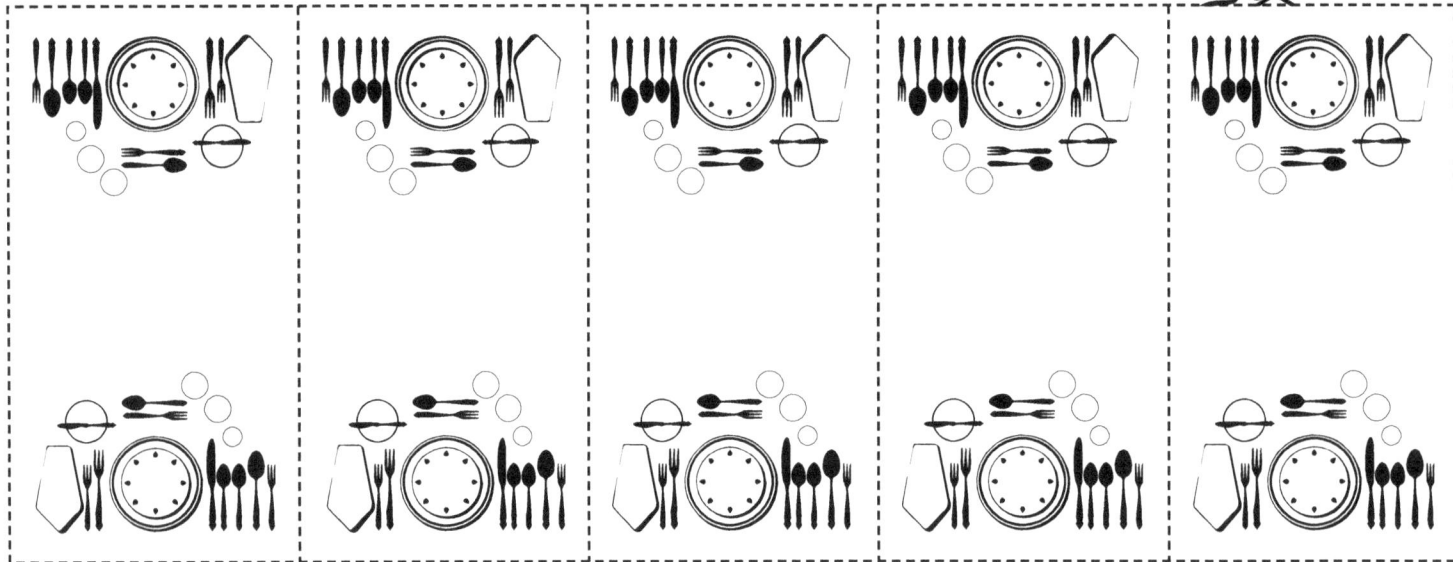

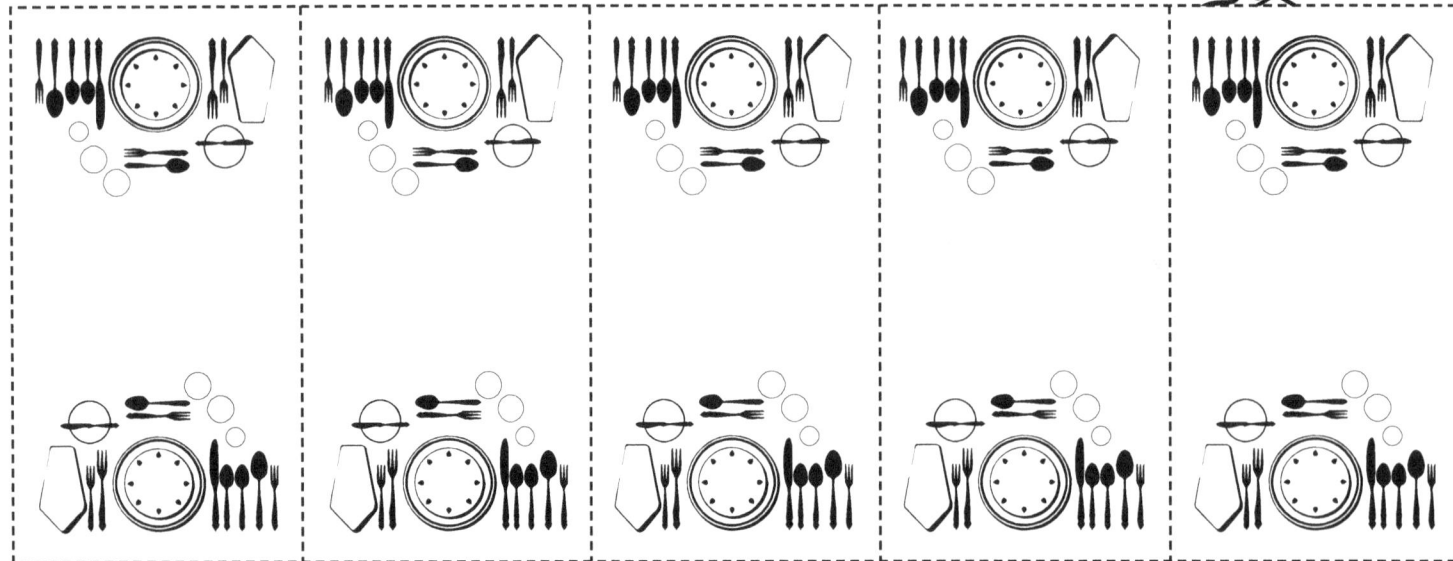

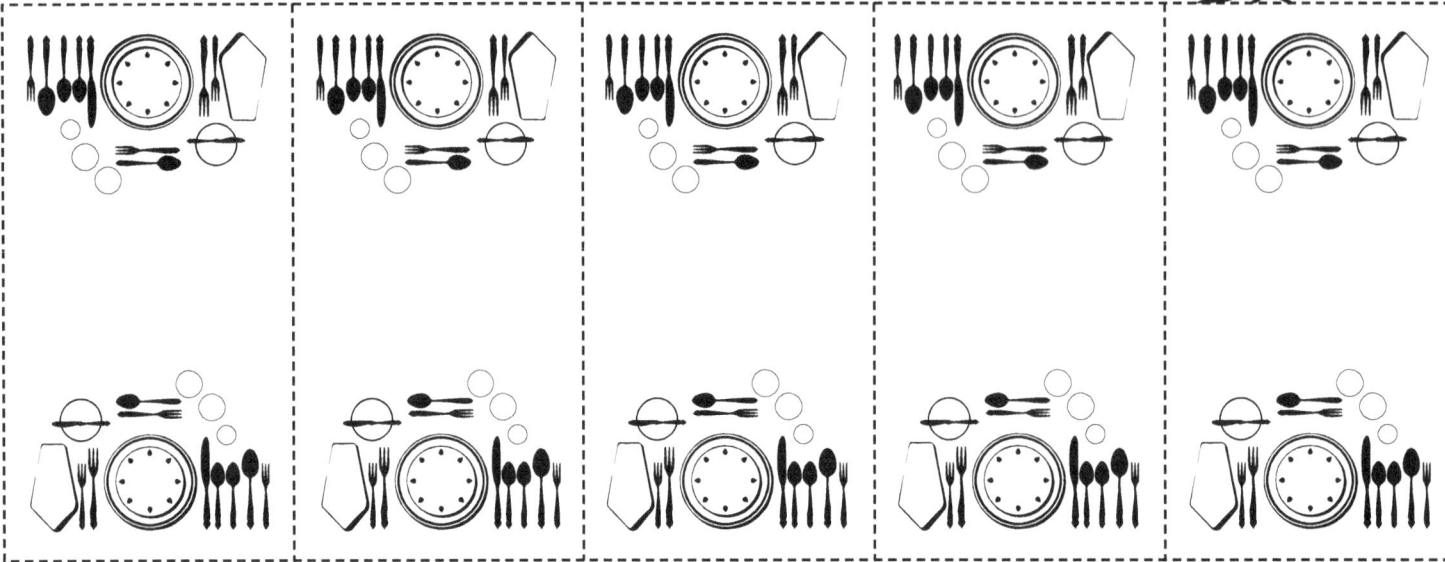

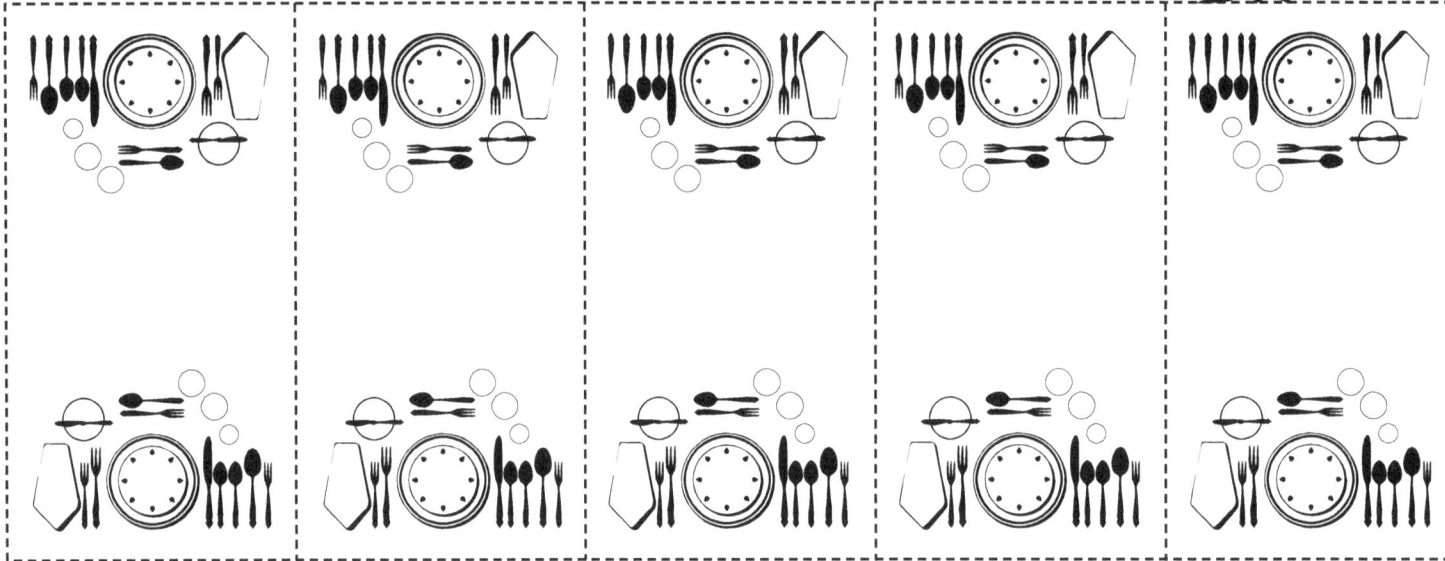

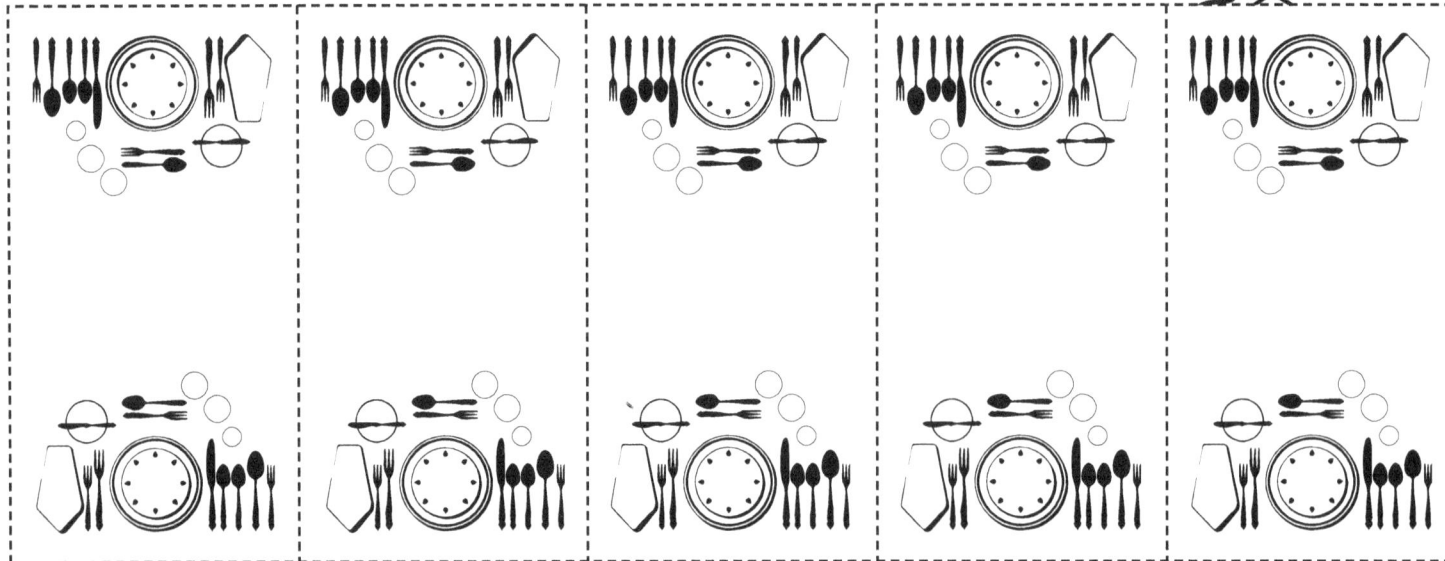

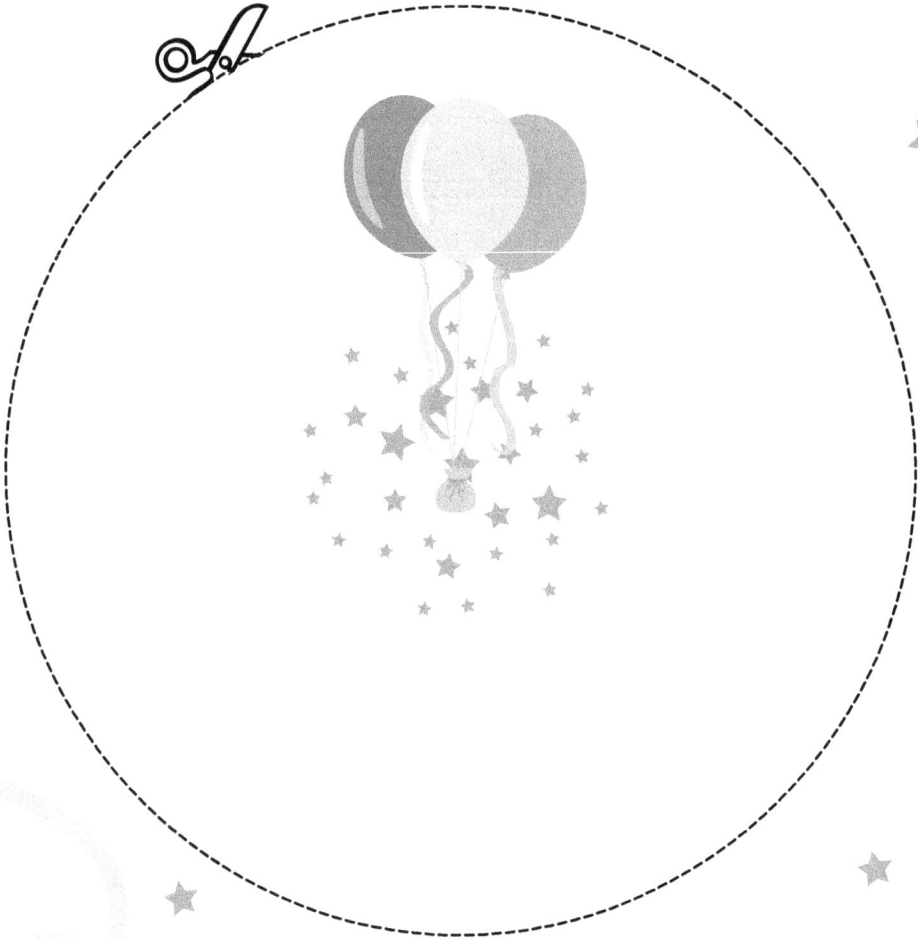

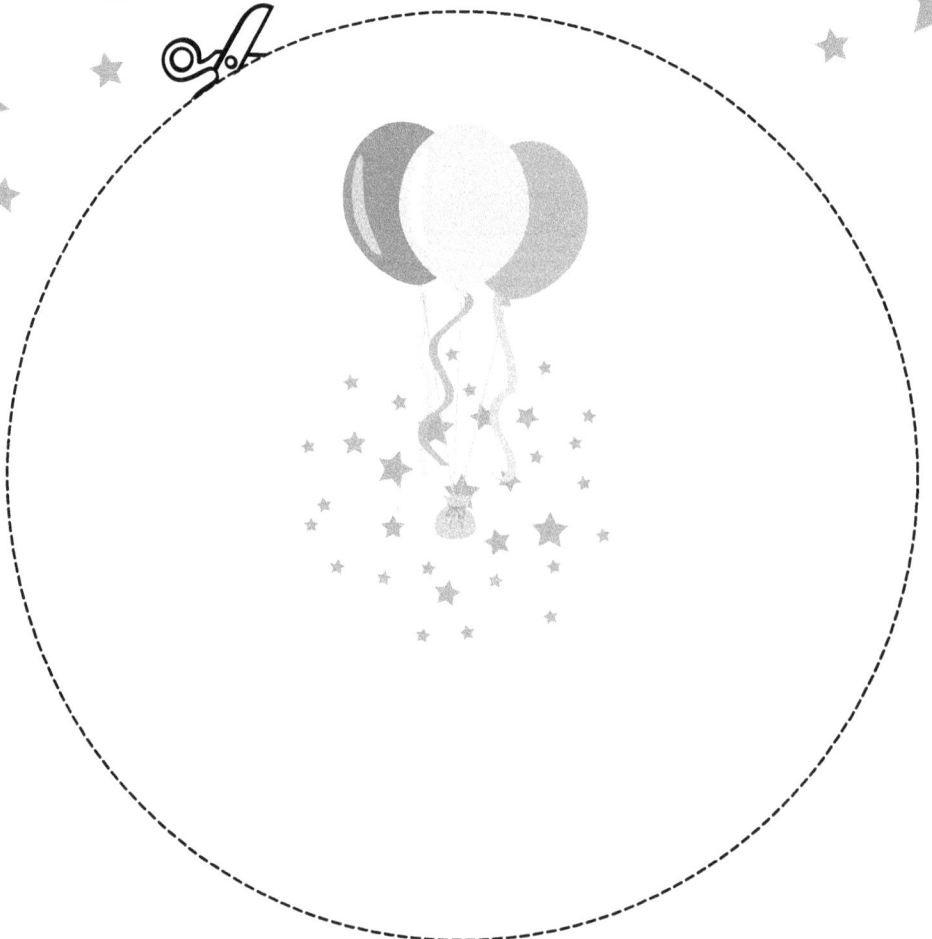

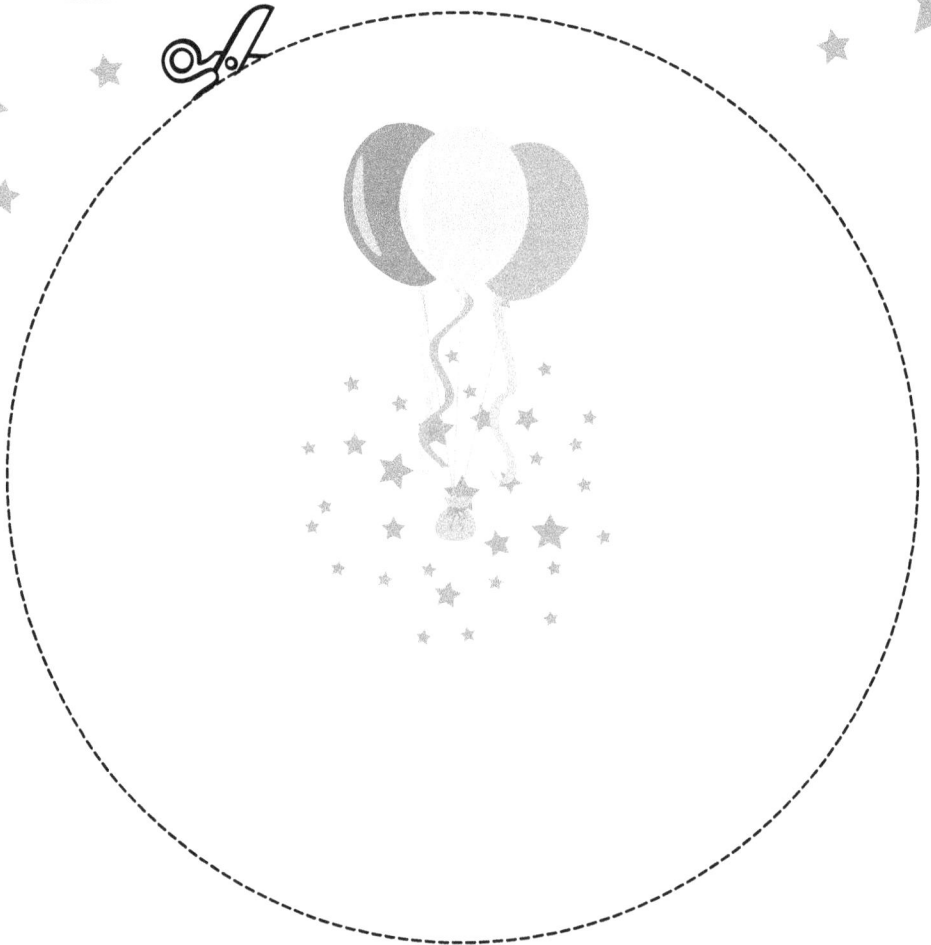

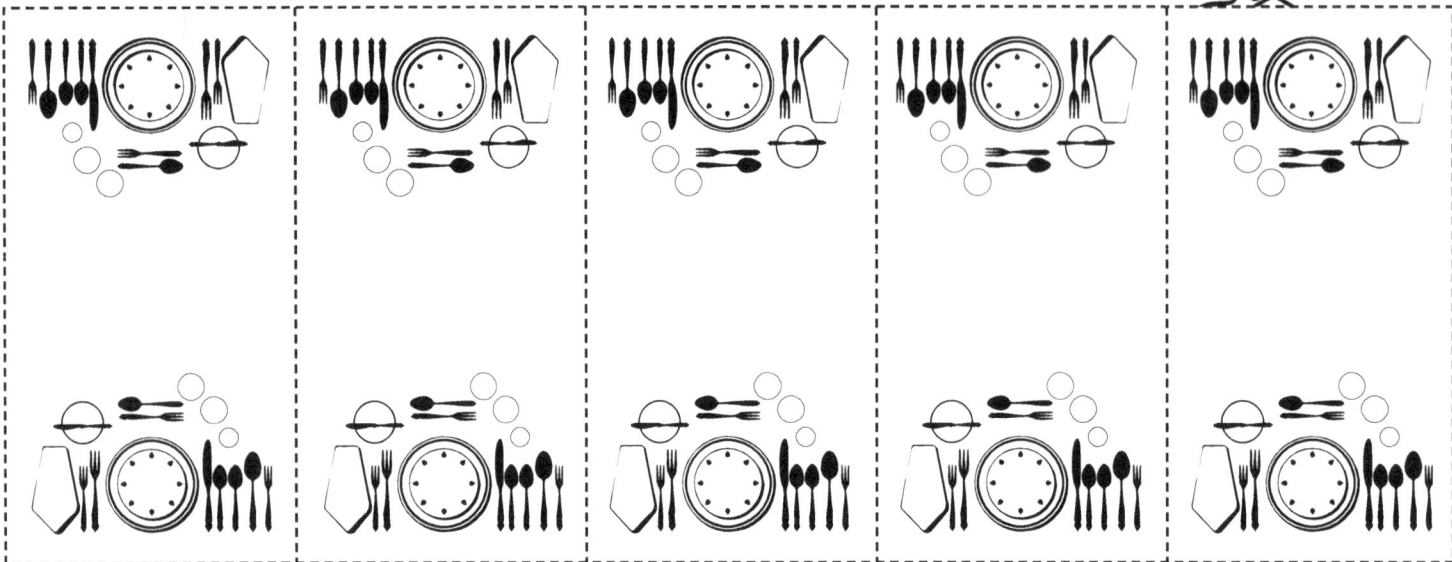

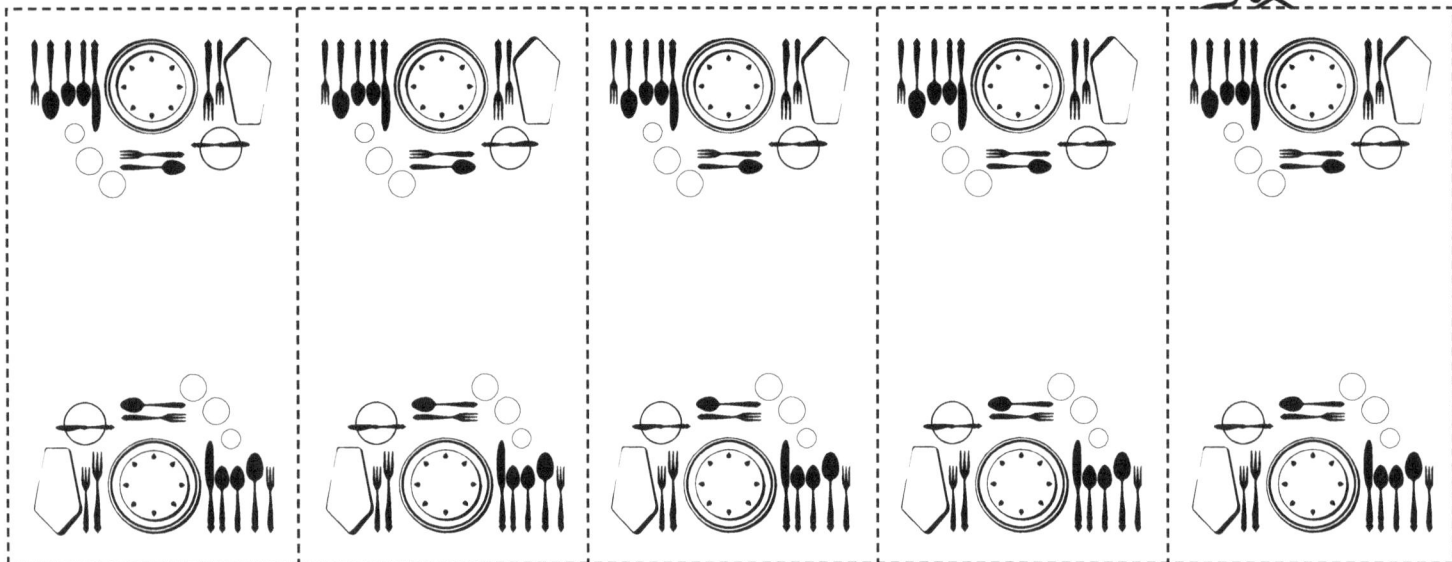

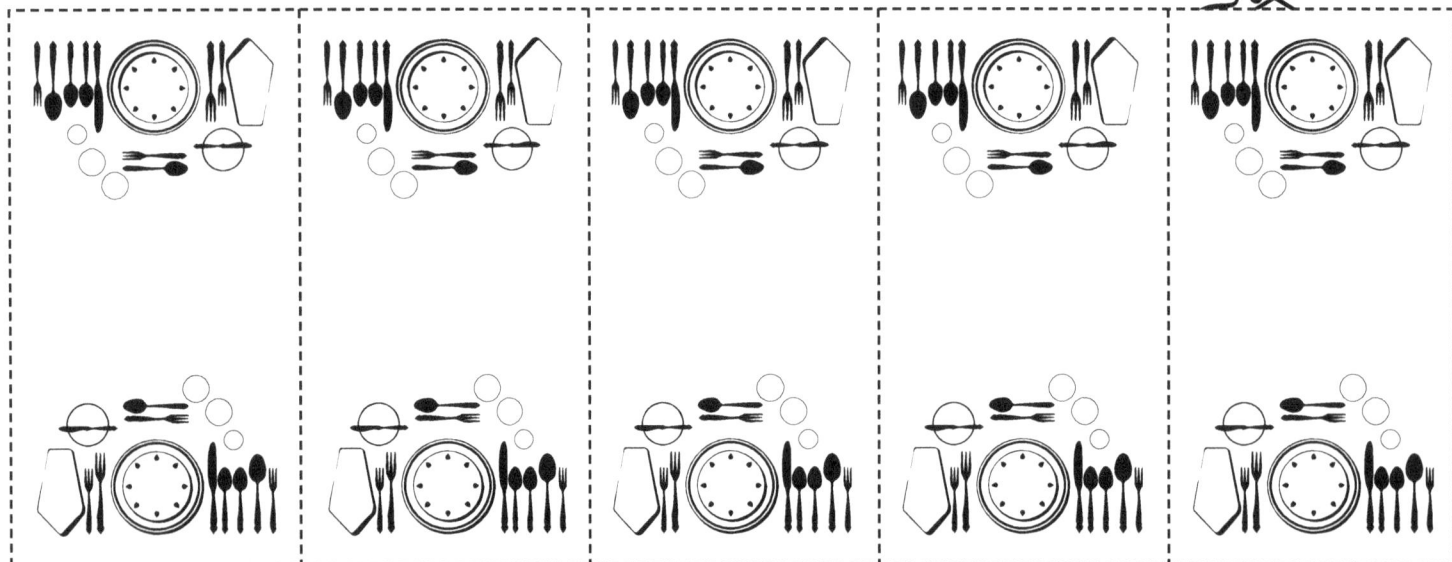

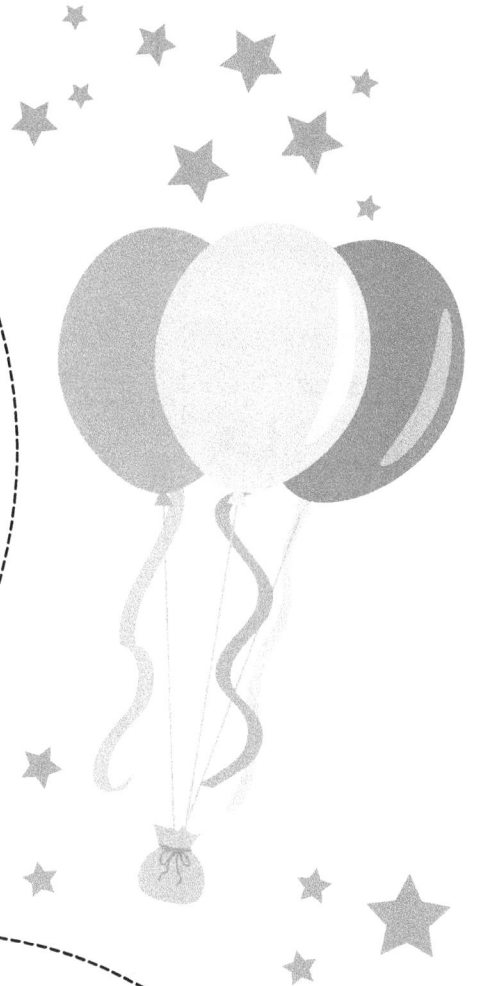

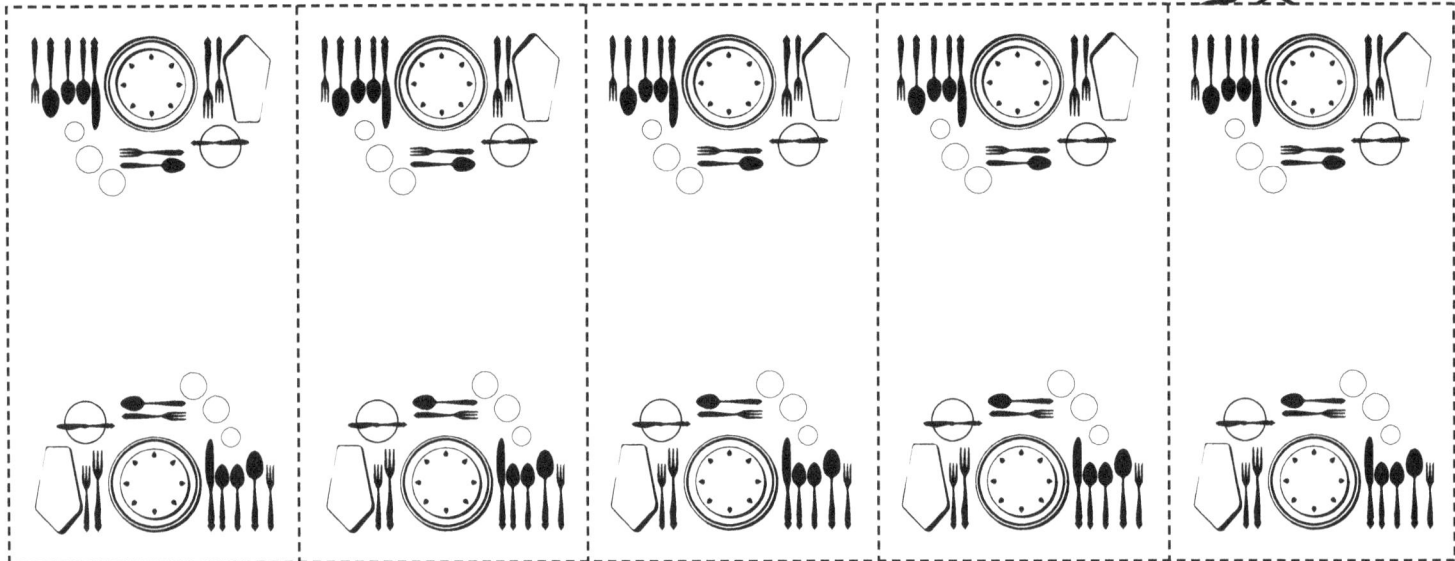

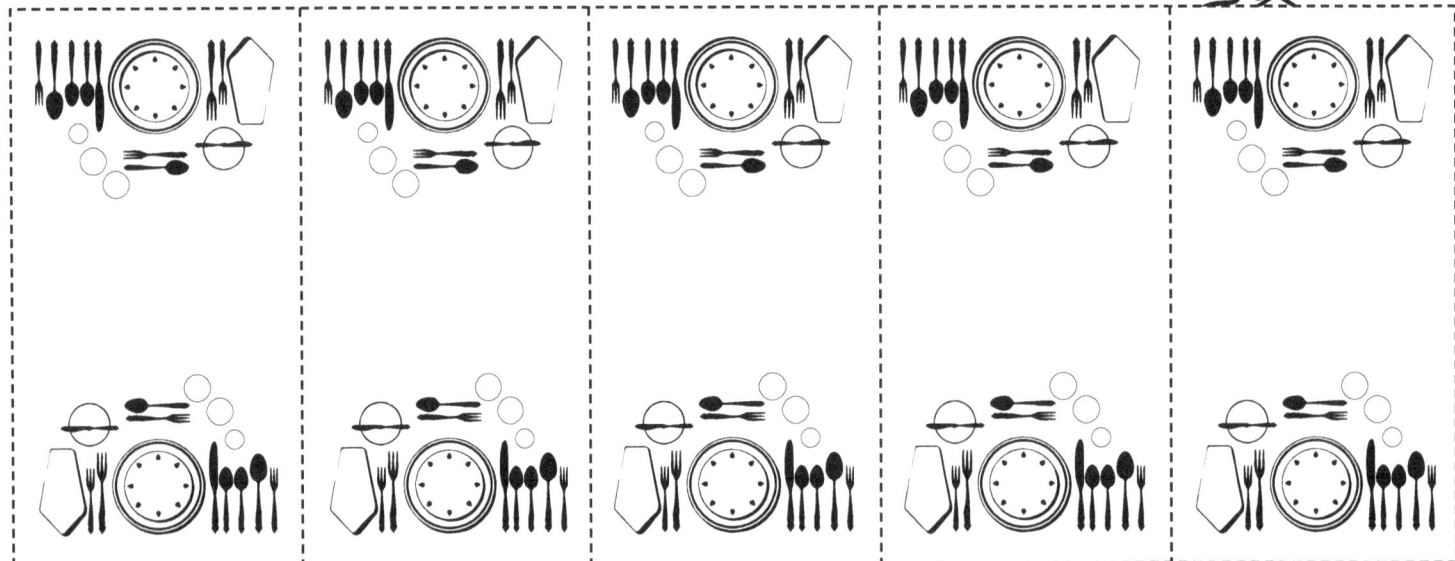

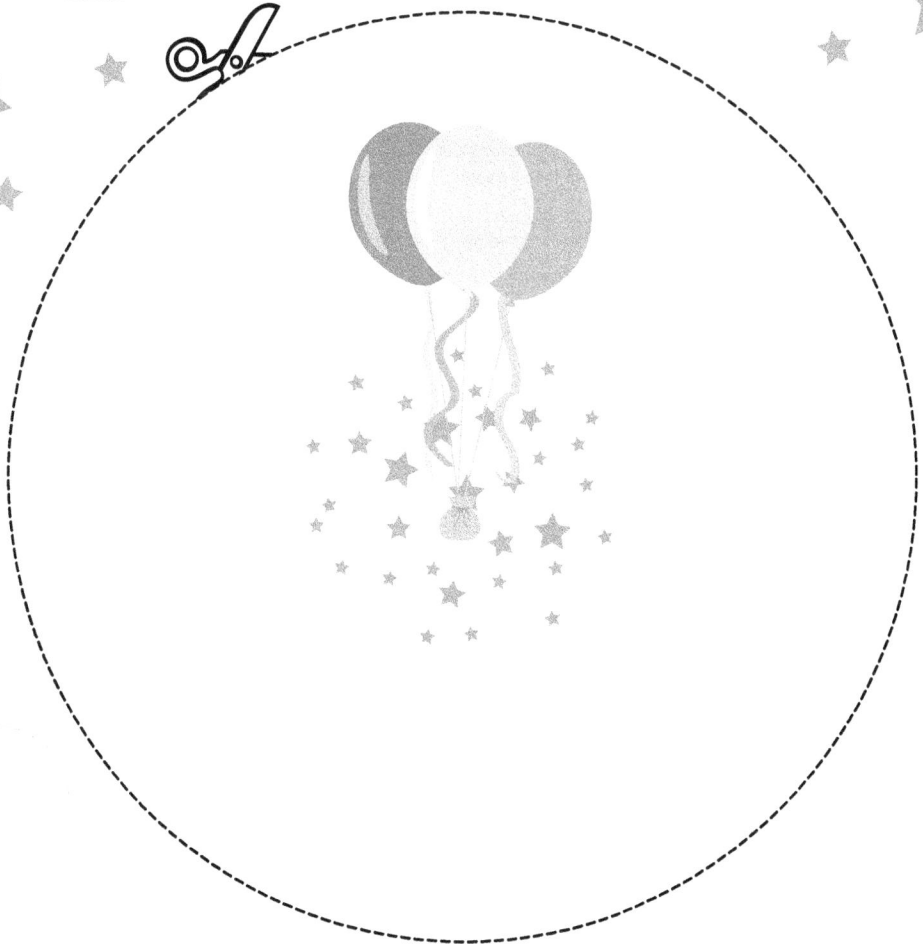

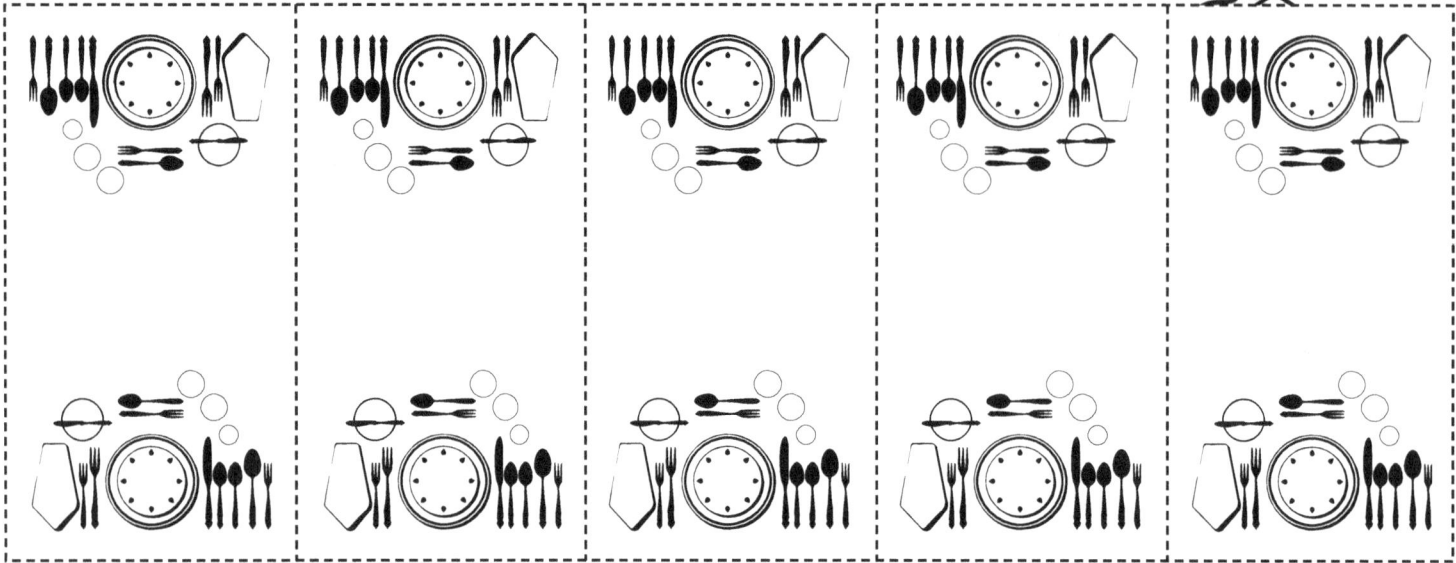

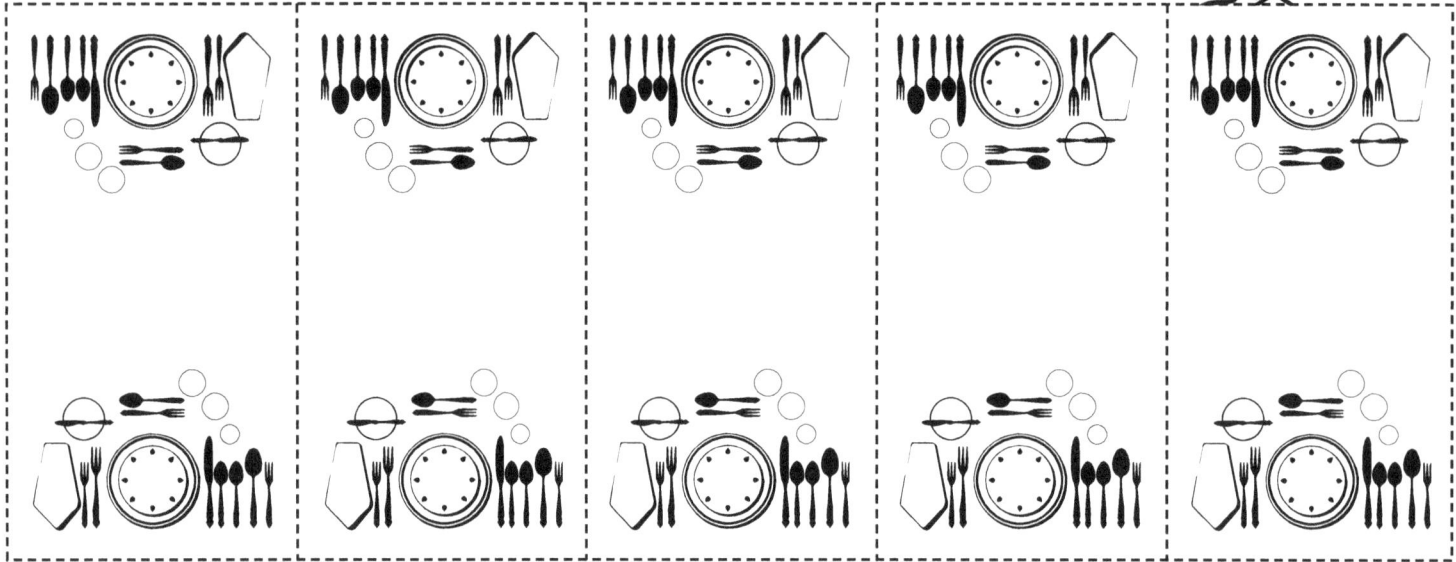

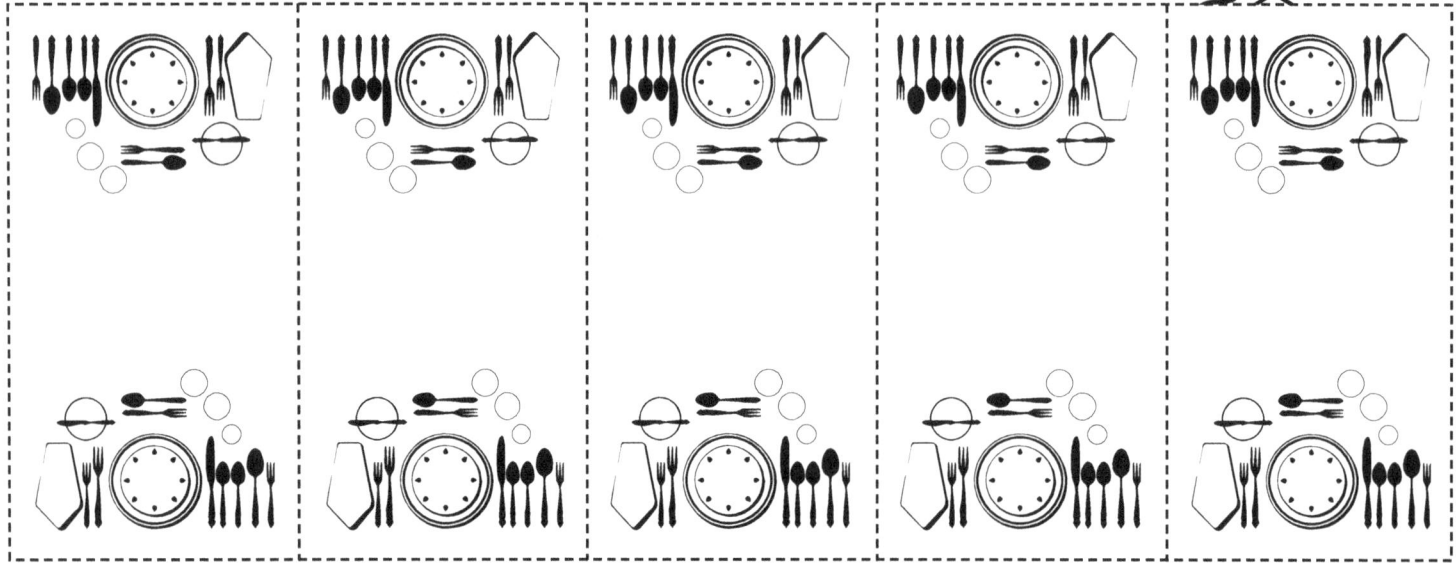

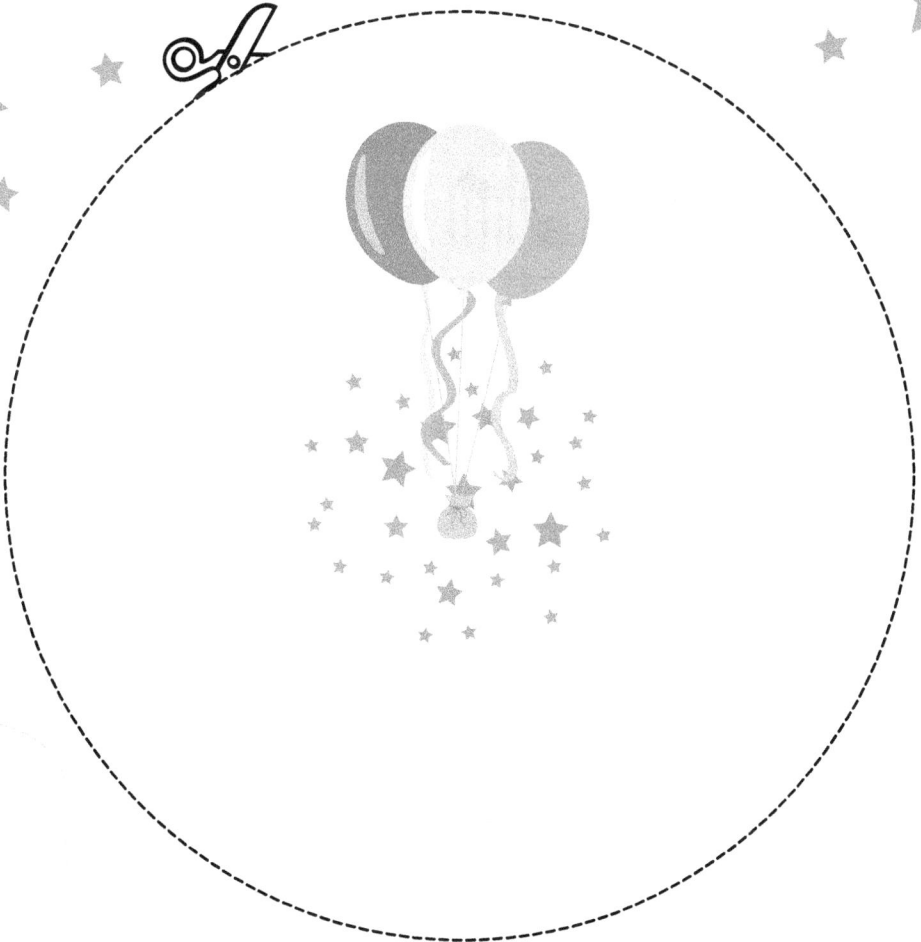

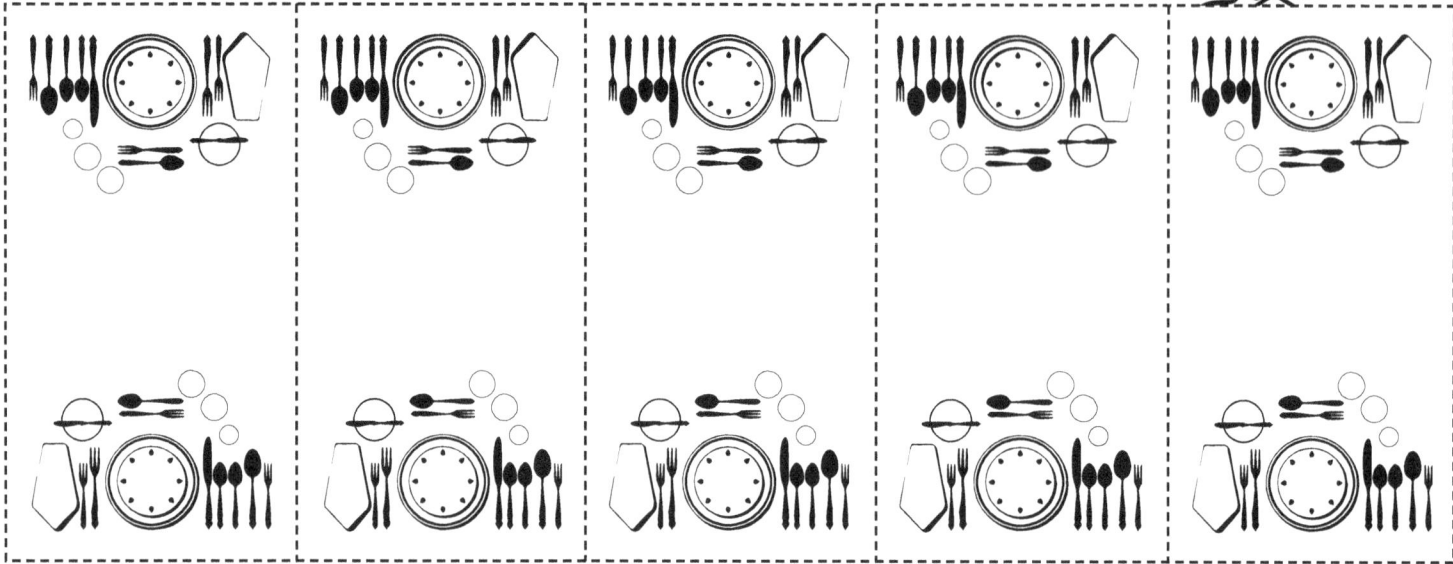

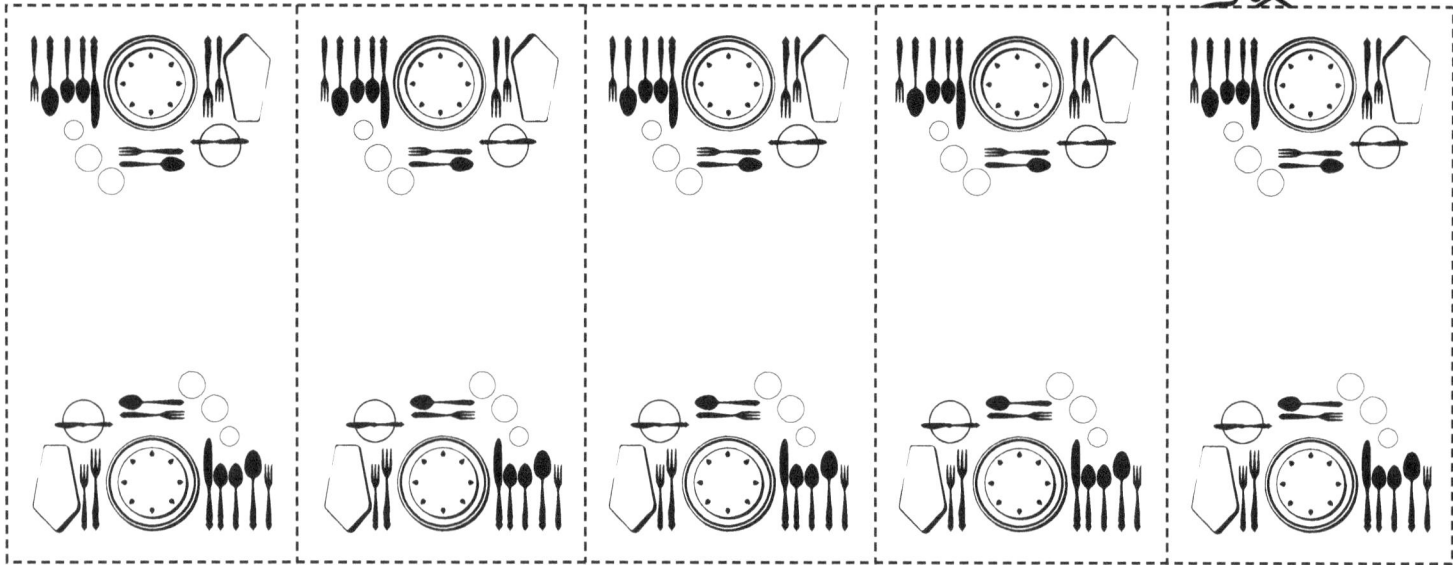

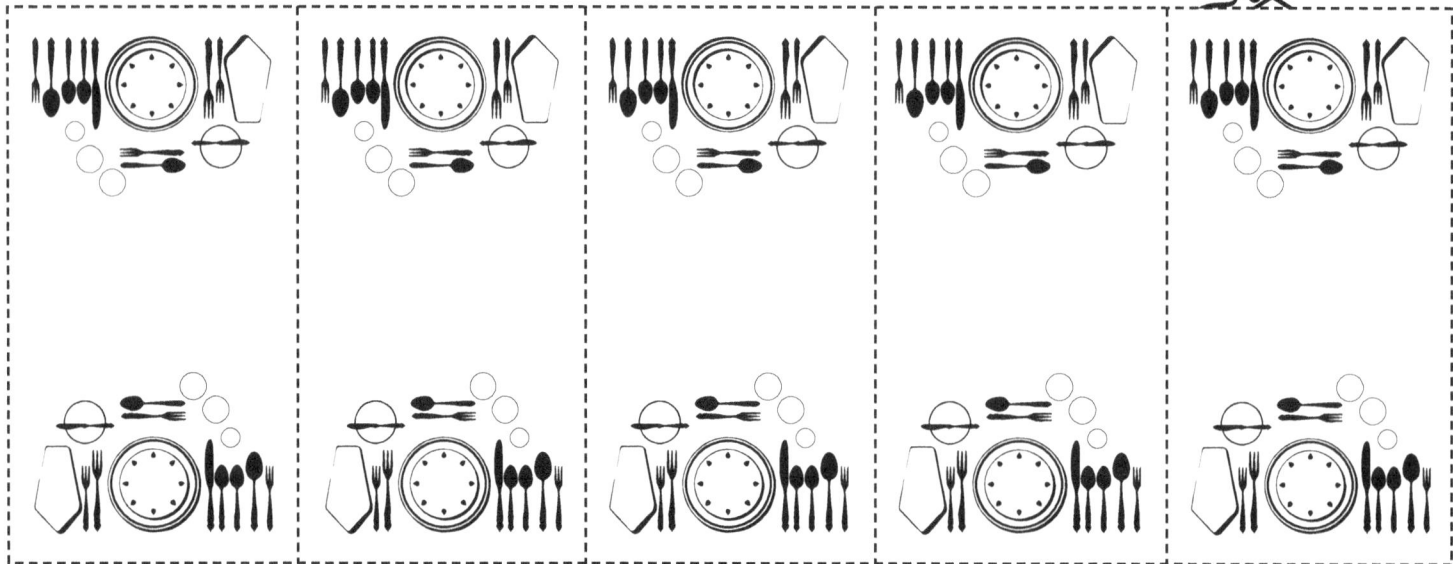

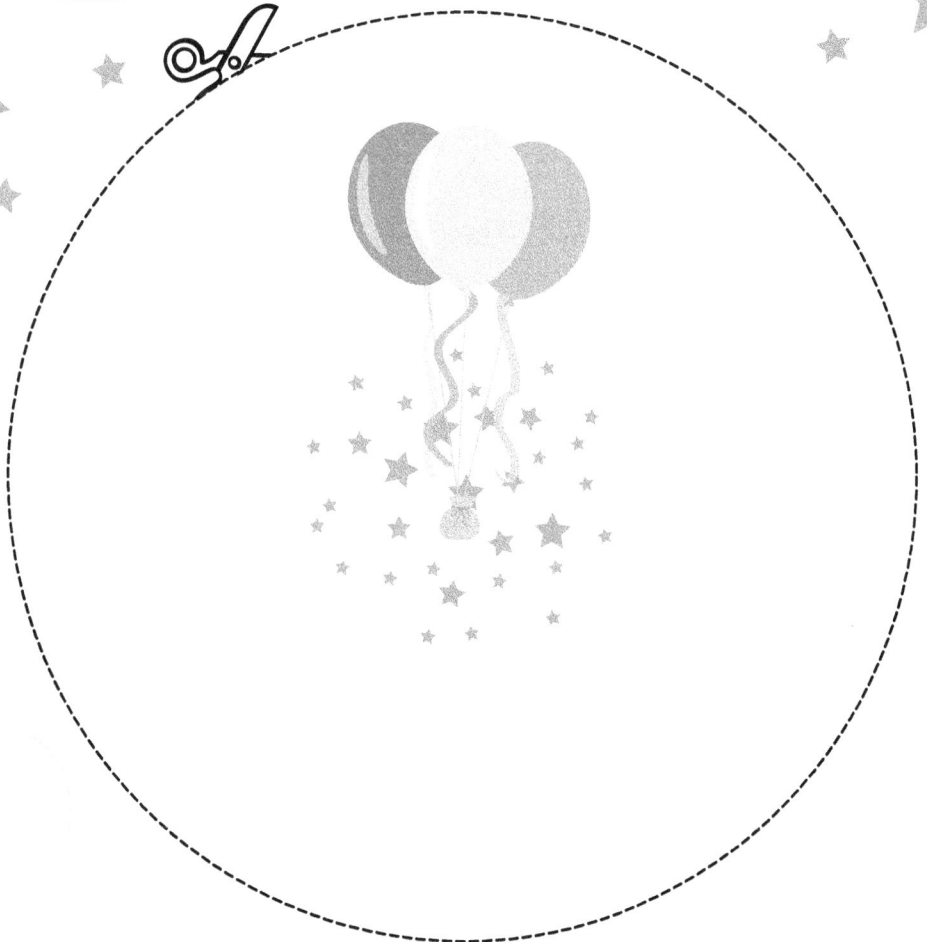

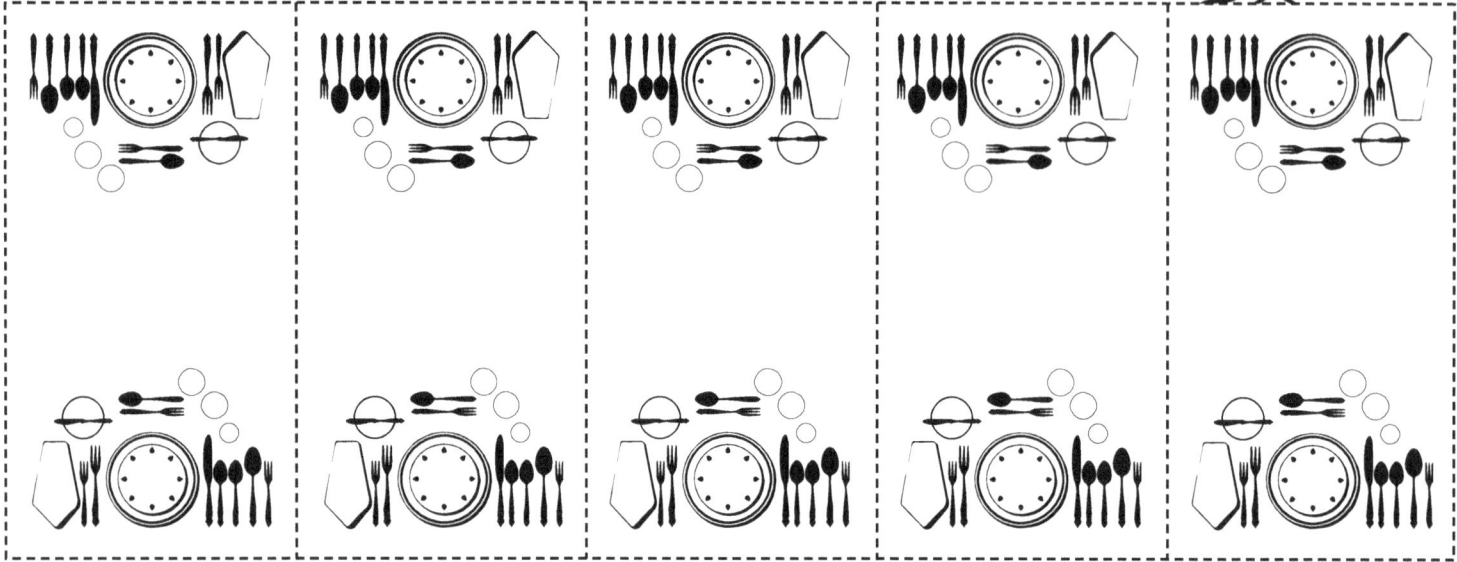

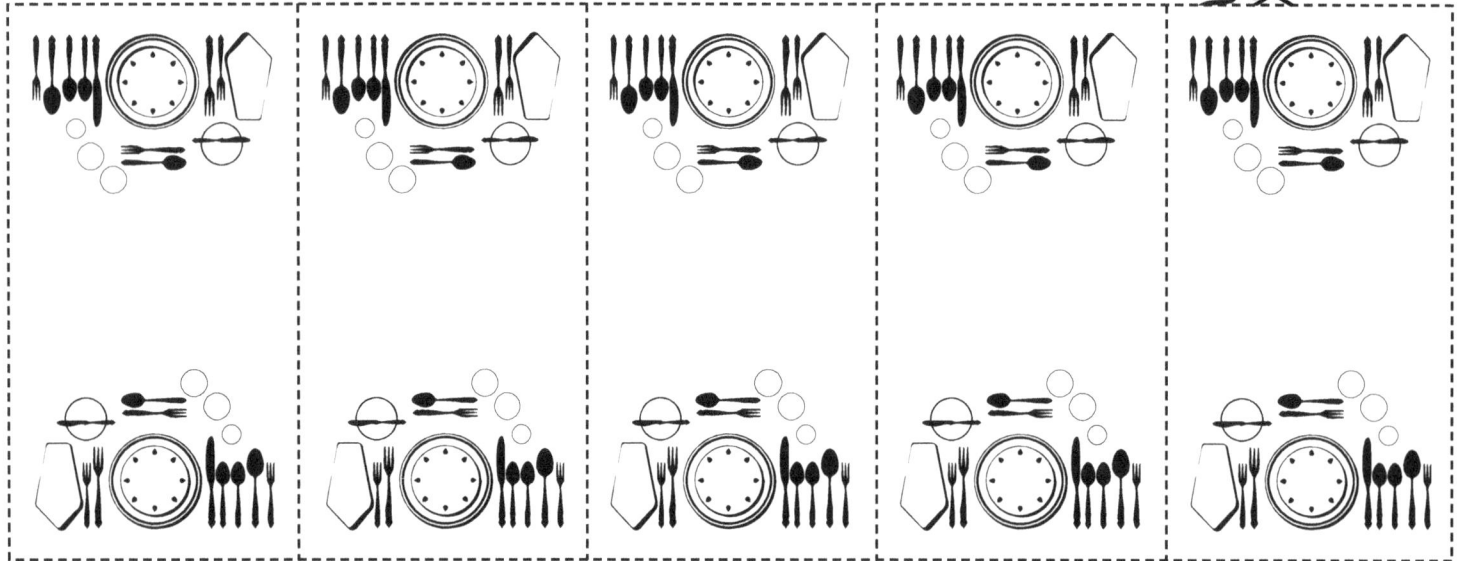

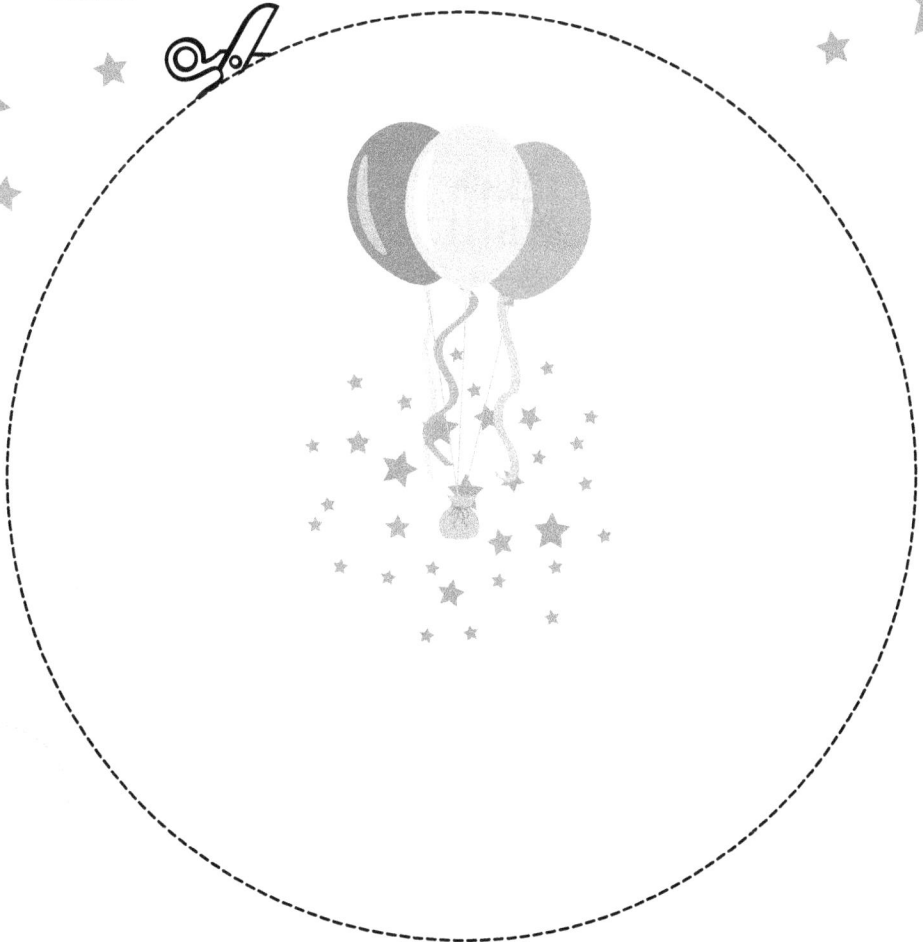

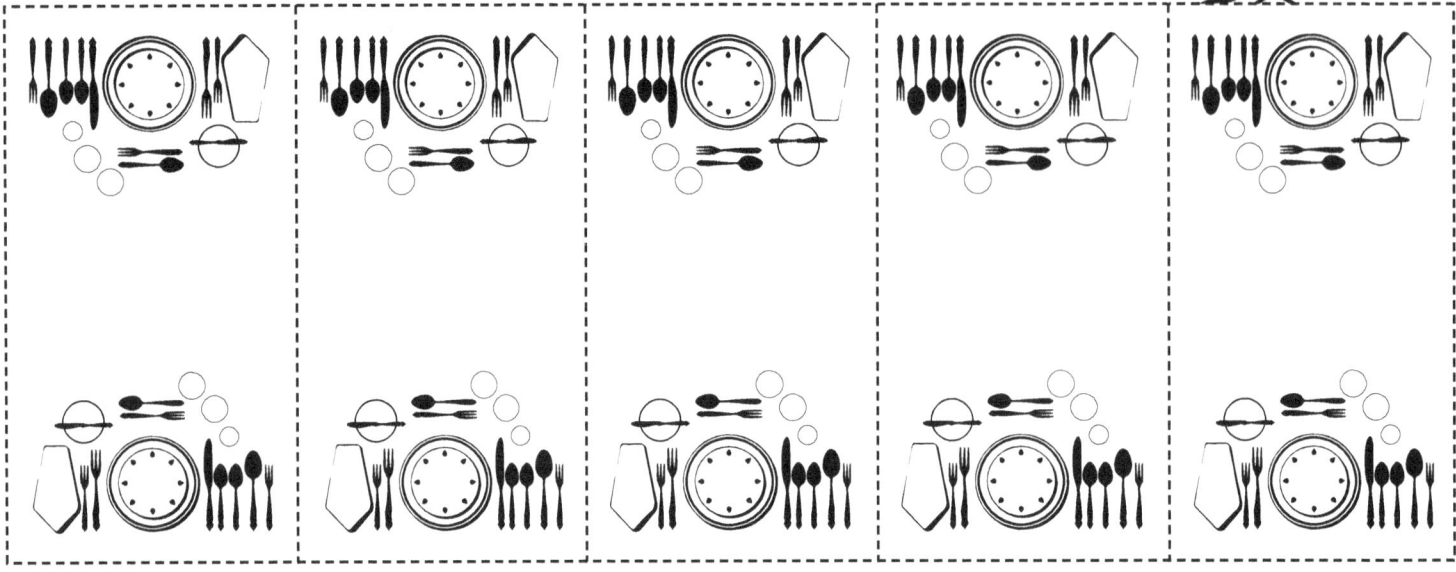

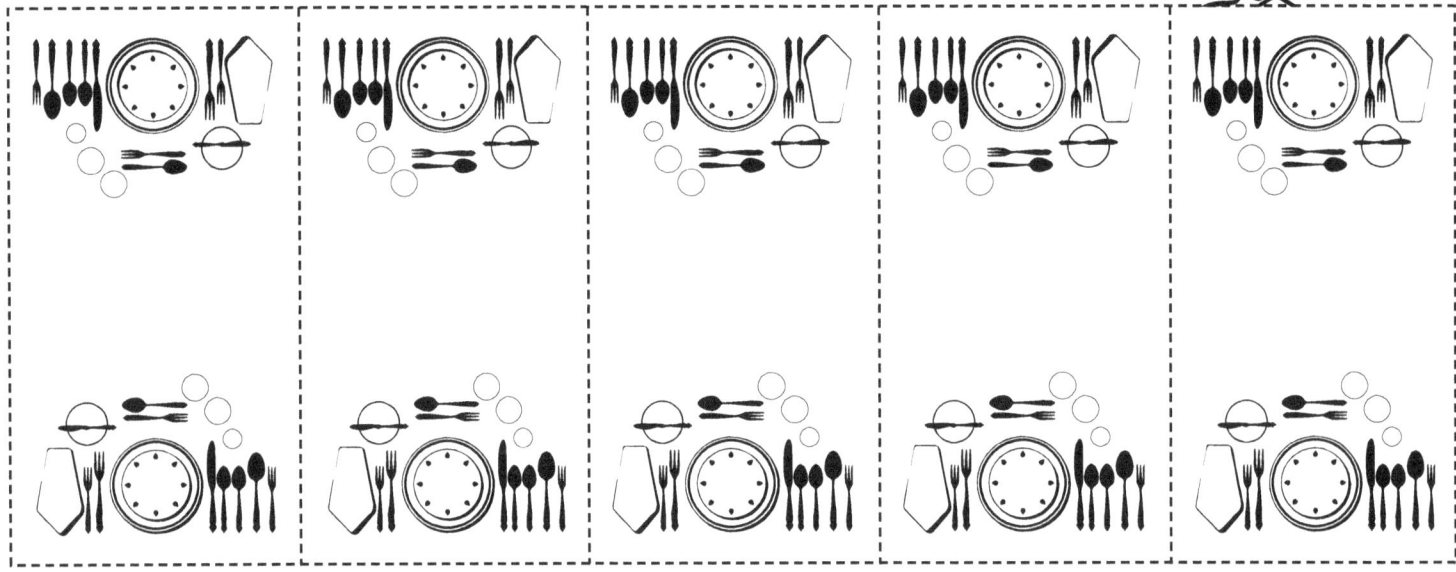

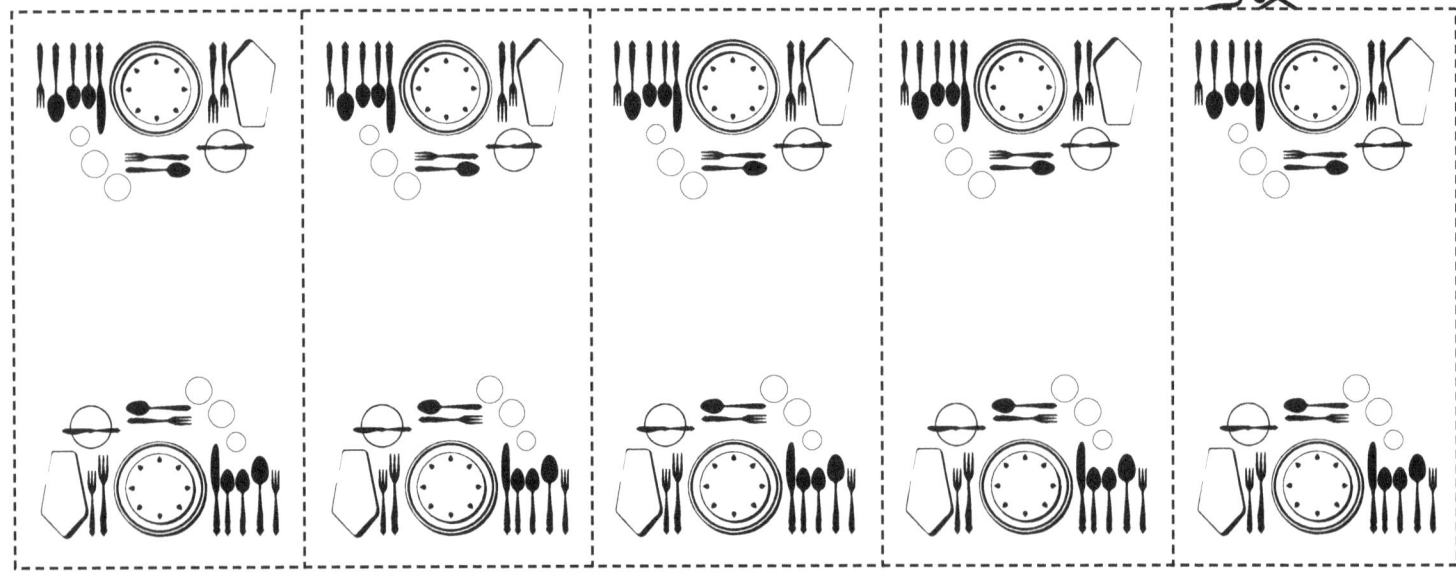

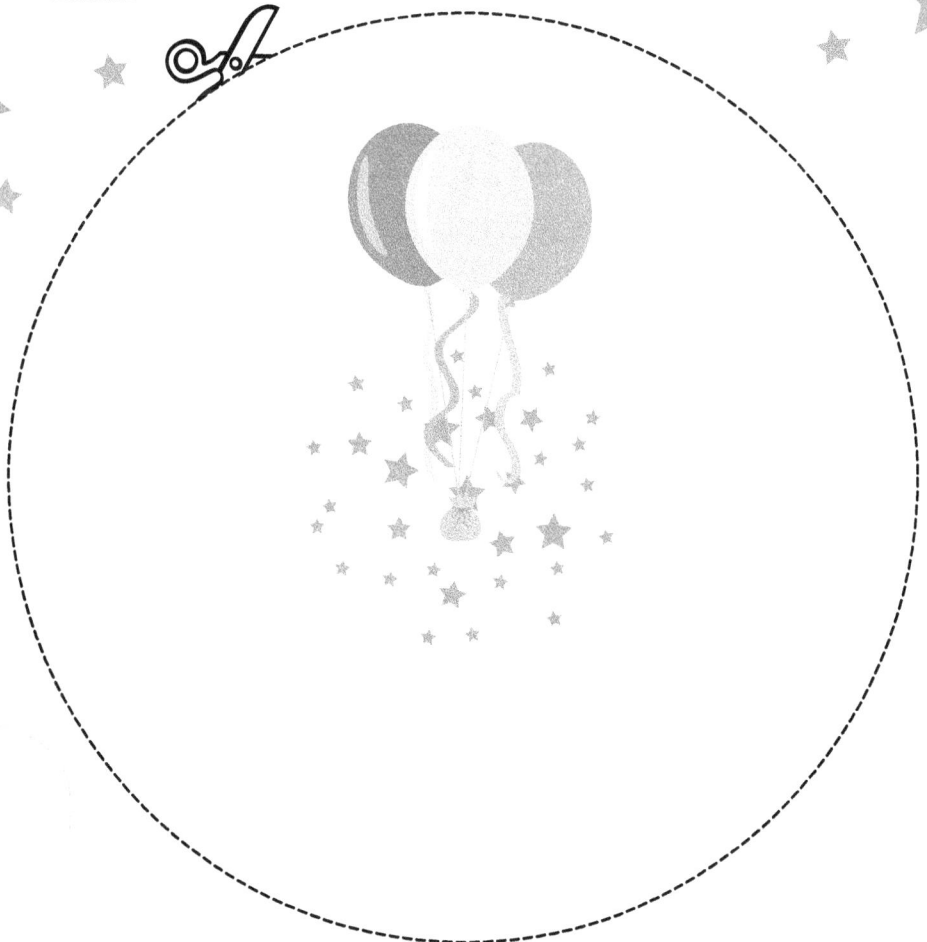

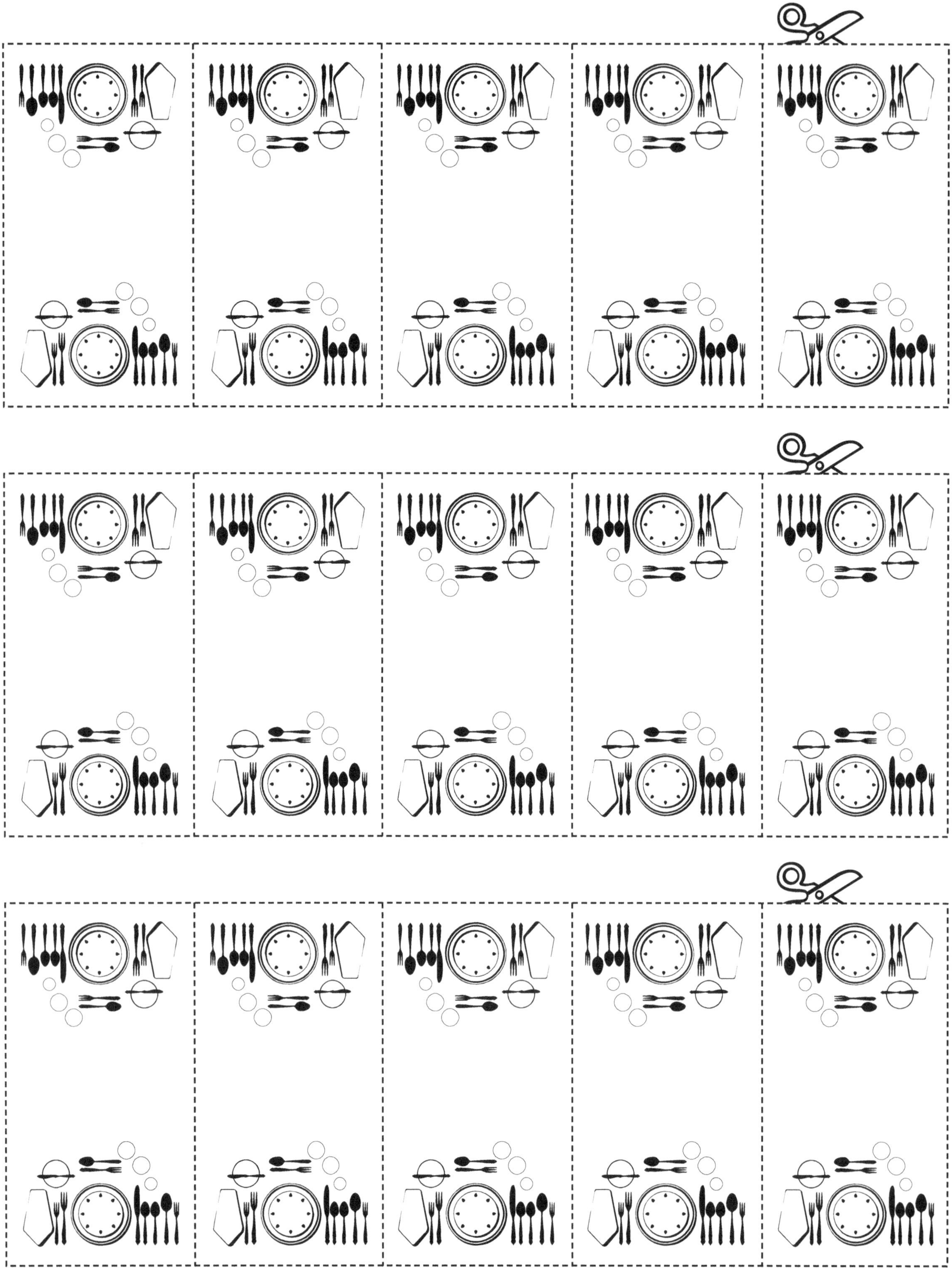

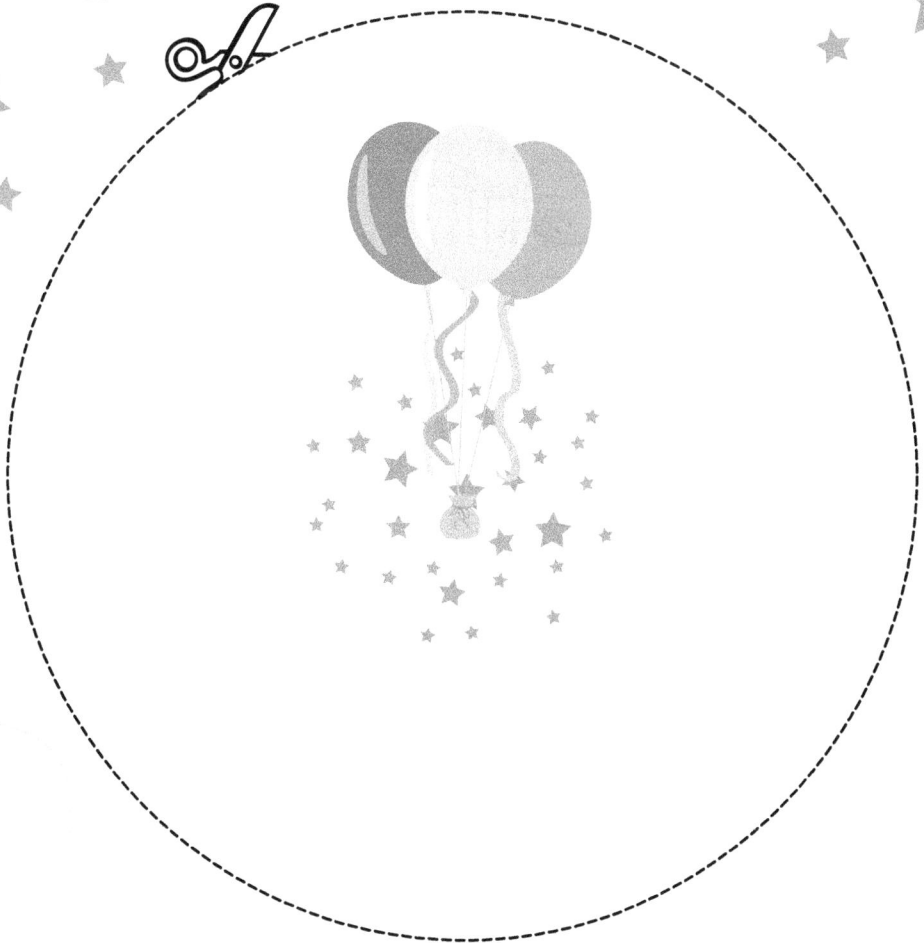

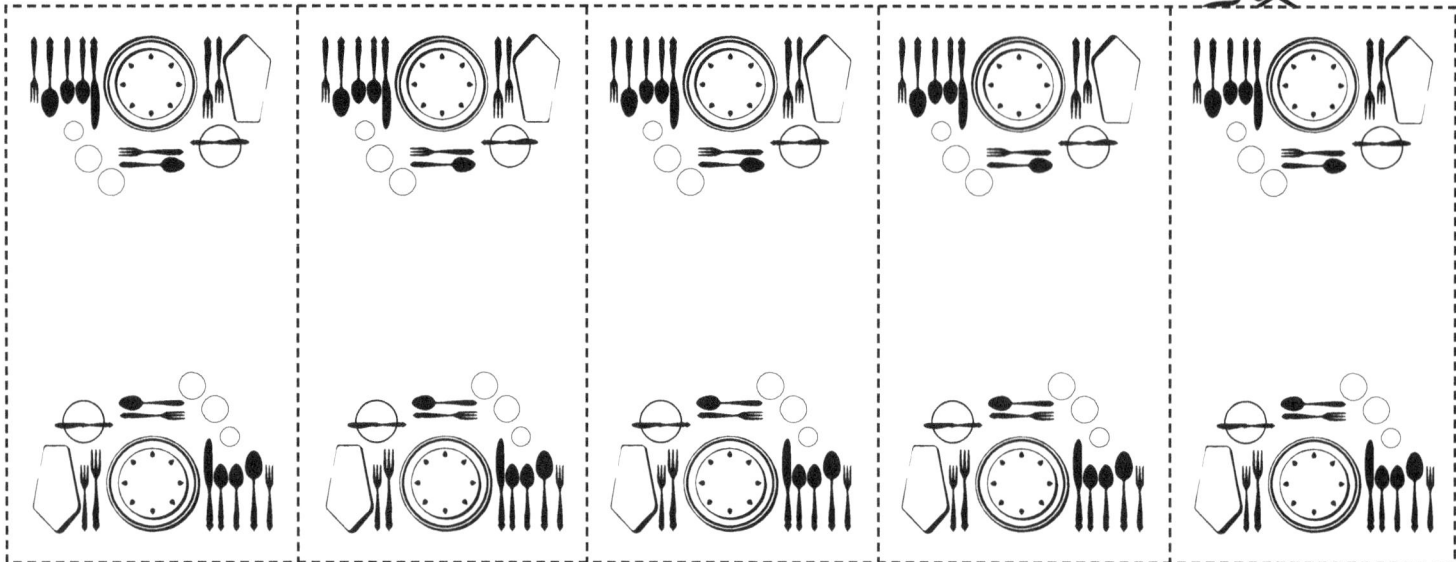

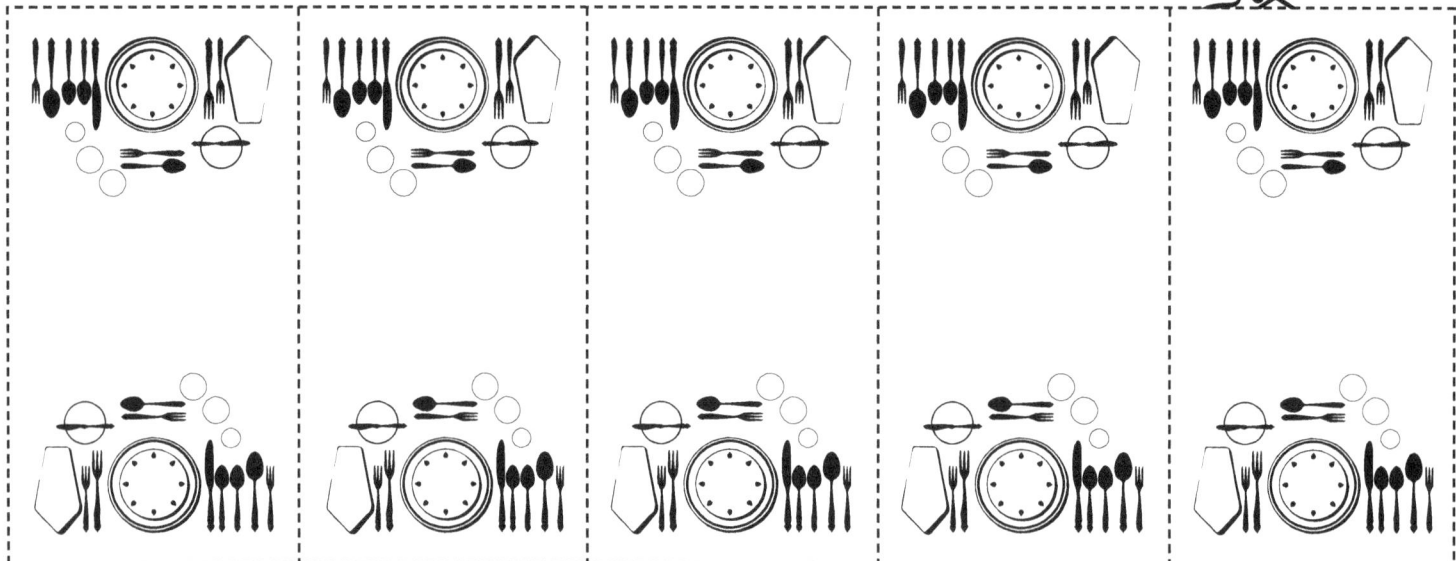

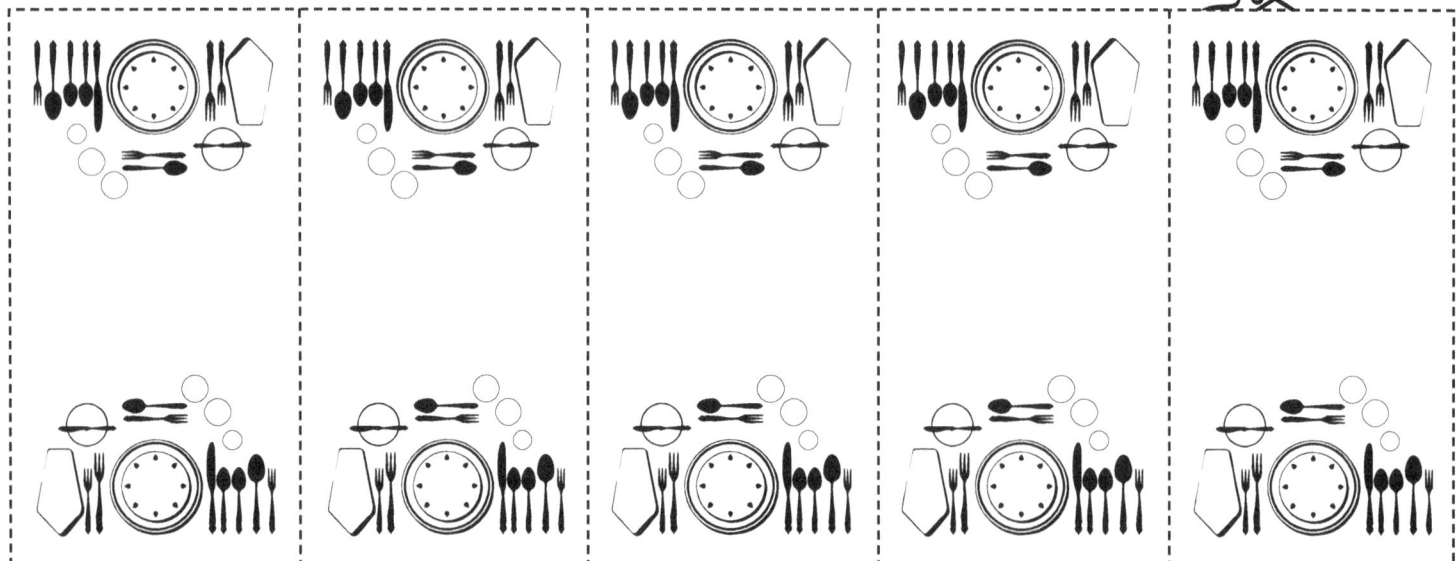

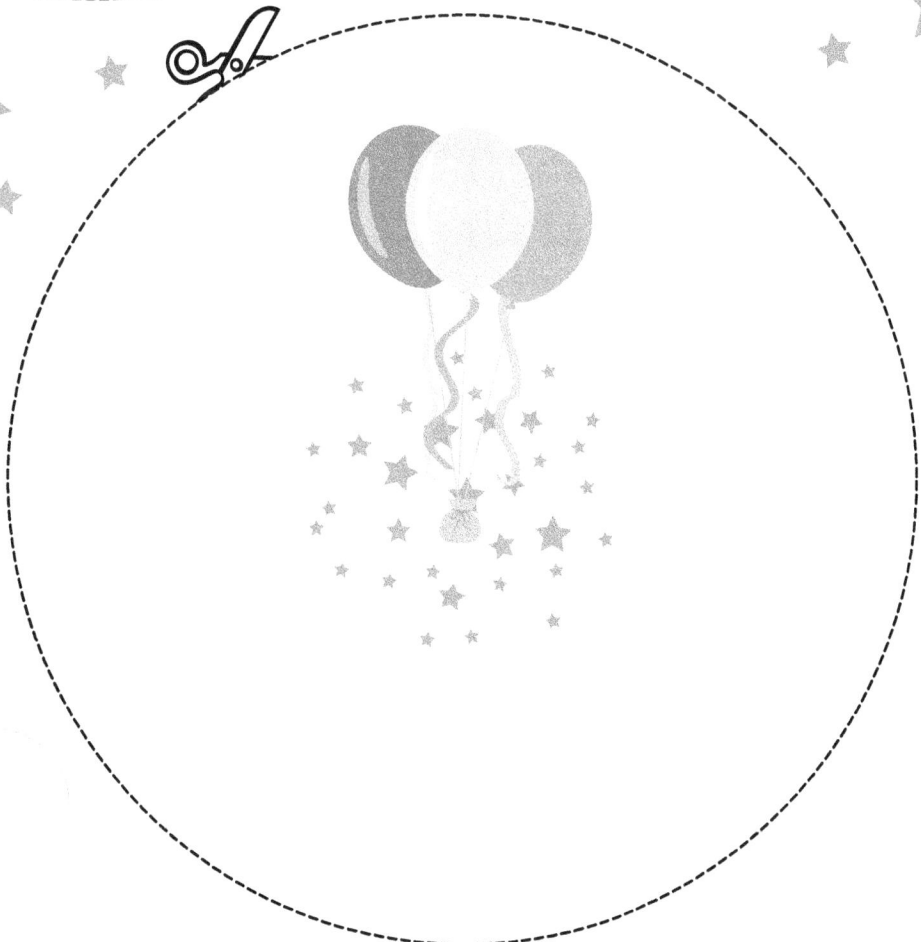

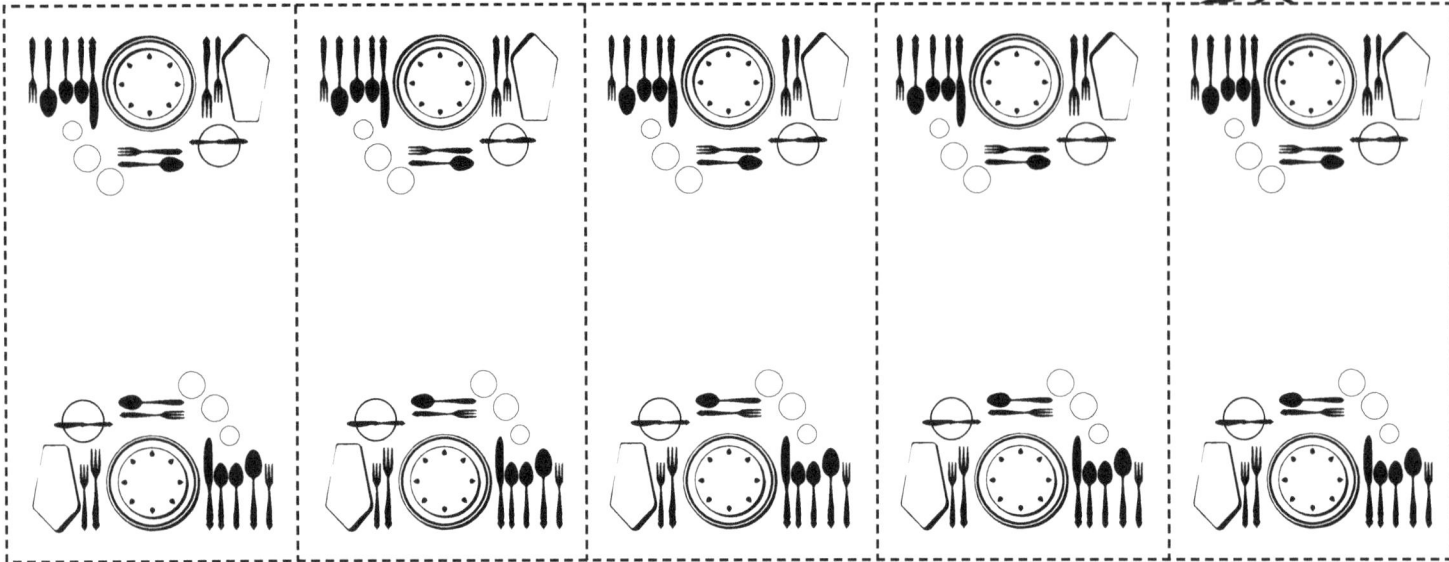

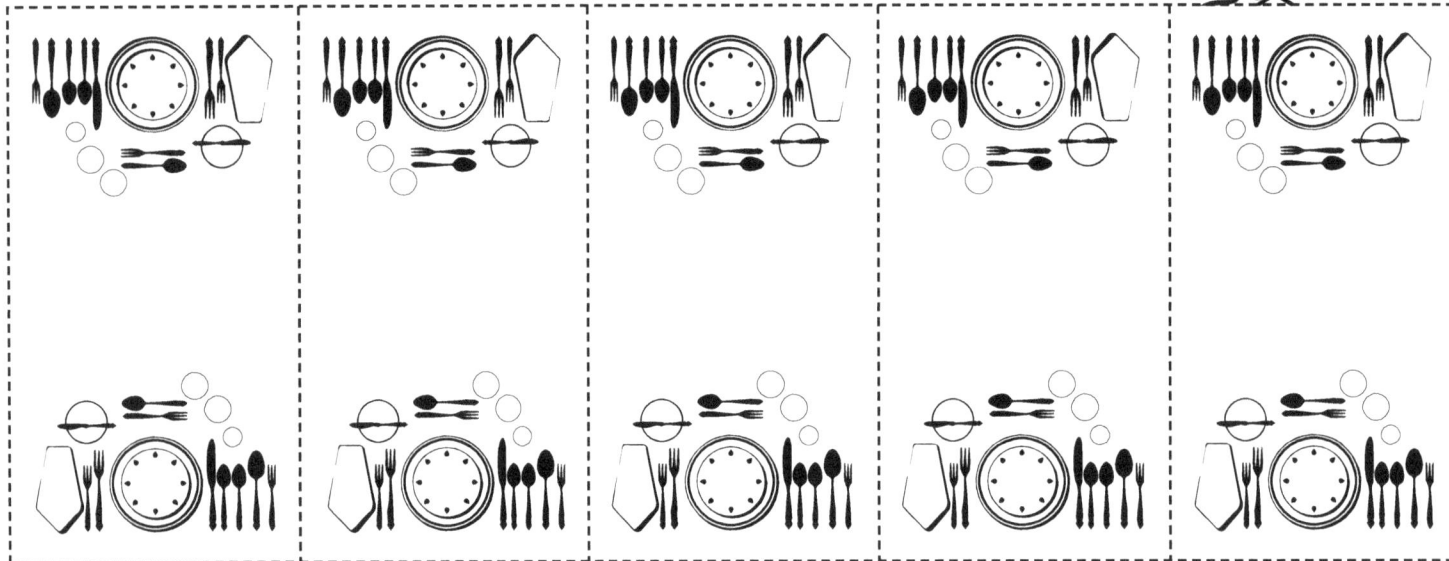

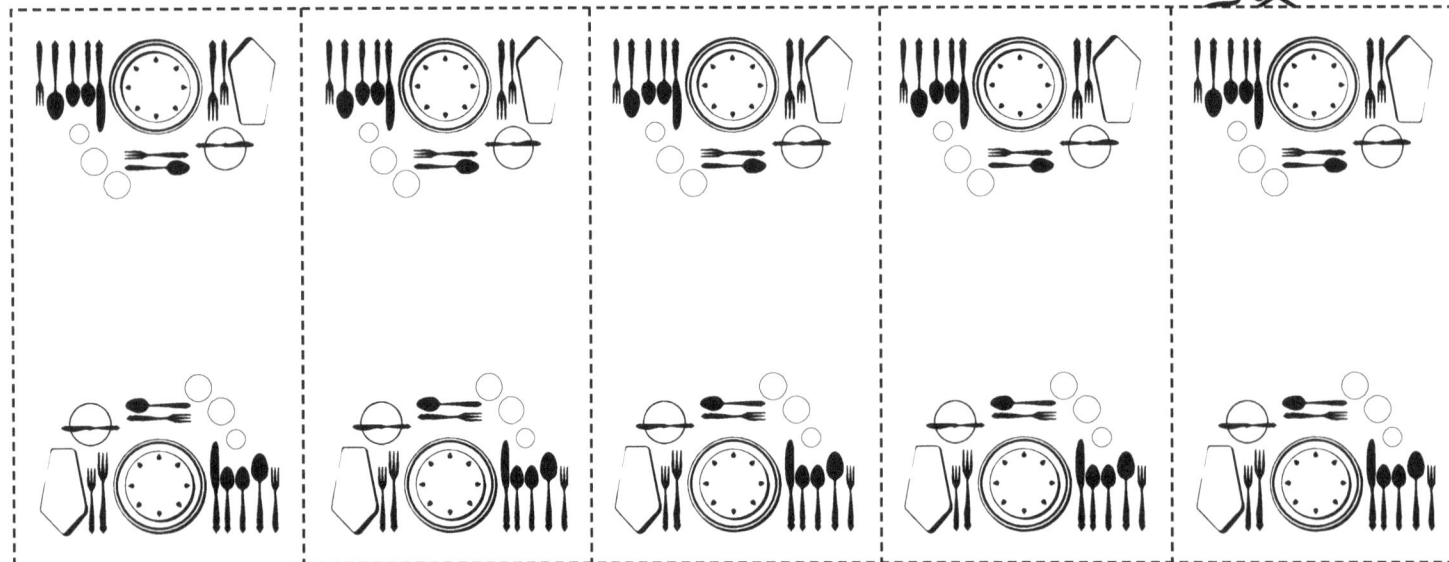

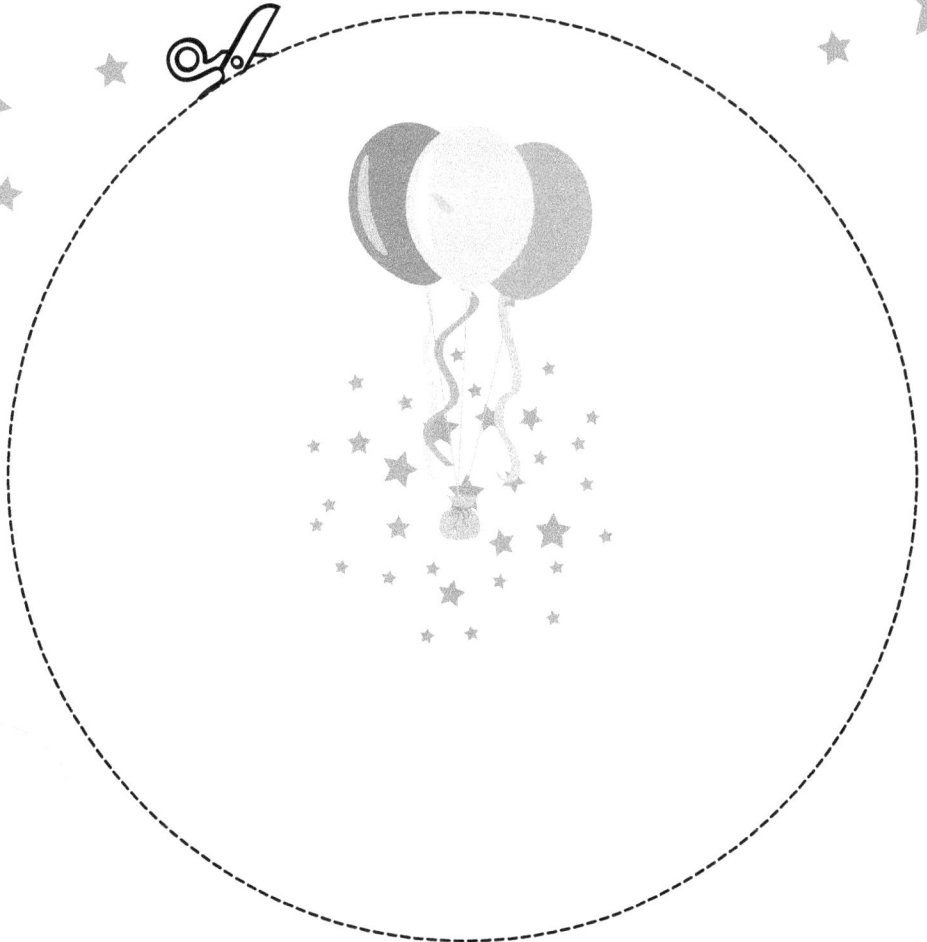

Final List Of Guests

Table 1

Table 2

Table 4

Table 4

Table 5

Table 6

Table 7

Table 8

Table 9

Table 10

Table 11

Table 12

Table 13

Table 14

Table 15

Table 16

Table 17

Table 18

Final Table Layout

Use this page to sketch out your ideal room layout.

www.ingramcontent.com/pod-product-compliance
Lightning Source LLC
Chambersburg PA
CBHW081233020426
42331CB00012B/3152